T0064824

THE
ULTIMATE GUIDE TO
SURVIVAL SHELTERS

THE
ULTIMATE GUIDE TO
SURVIVAL SHELTERS

HOW TO BUILD TEMPORARY
REFUGE IN ANY ENVIRONMENT

Tim MacWelch

Skyhorse Publishing

Copyright © 2021 by Tim MacWelch

All rights reserved. No part of this book may be reproduced in any manner without the
express written consent of the publisher, except in the case of brief excerpts in critical
reviews or articles. All inquiries should be addressed to Skyhorse Publishing, 307 West
36th Street, 11th Floor, New York, NY 10018.

Skyhorse Publishing books may be purchased in bulk at special discounts for sales
promotion, corporate gifts, fund-raising, or educational purposes. Special editions
can also be created to specifications. For details, contact the Special Sales Department,
Skyhorse Publishing, 307 West 36th Street, 11th Floor, New York, NY 10018 or
info@skyhorsepublishing.com.

Skyhorse® and Skyhorse Publishing® are registered trademarks of Skyhorse Publishing,
Inc.®, a Delaware corporation.

Visit our website at www.skyhorsepublishing.com.

10 9 8 7 6 5 4 3 2 1

Library of Congress Cataloging-in-Publication Data is available on file.

Cover design by Kai Texel

Print ISBN: 978-1-5107-5556-7
Ebook ISBN: 978-1-5107-5847-6

Printed in China

Table of Contents

Introduction

What does it mean to have "shelter," and why is it such an important survival commodity? Even further, does your dwelling have to possess an asphalt-shingled roof overhead (and a big fat mortgage payment), or can this refuge be something far simpler and more expedient?

If coziness is the measure of shelter, then the average modern home is the benchmark to hit. With insulated windows, lights that come on at the flick of a switch, and climate-controlled air that we can adjust on a whim, the typical house is a place of great comfort and a haven from the extremes of nature. Whether this home is a condo, townhouse, or mansion, each one has systems in place that create a highly comfortable atmosphere, especially when compared to the rude cabins, shacks, and huts of our predecessors. But what if I told you that you could survive without that comfortable home? It's true. In fact, you can subsist with a lot less than you'd expect.

When it comes down to a question of survival over comfort, all we really have to do is keep our body temperature close enough to a healthy range and receive protection from the hazards of the area.

These parameters make the term "shelter" much broader and allow it to fit a wide range of protective structures and assets, both natural and man-made. Again, if comfort takes a backseat to basic survival, a damp cave, a cheap tent, or an abandoned car are all capable of providing us with shelter. That's a good thing, too.

Shelter can come in many forms, and unless you're in imminent danger (such as bleeding heavily or having a respiratory problem), acquiring shelter is going to be your top priority in an emergency situation. Certainly, if a bear is about to eat you, or you're sliding off a cliff,, you've got bigger problems than "exposure" to heat or cold; however, when you're not under the threat of beasts or bleeding out, shelter is the thing you need most. And even though food and water may seem just as vital to the average person, or even more important than shelter, we have to put it all into perspective. While we can go without a drop of water for days, we can also go with only water (no food) for weeks before *Death* comes to collect us. Yet in extreme cold, or high heat, we may not last more than a few hours—even if we had all the food and water in the world. In the first chapter of this book, we'll discuss the dangers of hypothermia, hyperthermia, and other environmental hazards, but for now, understand this: Shelter doesn't have to come in the form of a mansion. All you really need is something to block the elements that would take your body temperature out of a safe range and can defend you from any creatures or conditions that would cause you harm. Thankfully for us, these simple protections can come from a surprising number of sources. Get ready to think of "shelter" in a whole new way!

1

Understand the Threats

Before we worry too much about survival shelter architecture and improvised building materials, it's important to understand all of the reasons we need shelter. As a species, we tend to think of ourselves as the dominant creature on this planet, and we often ignore our physical limitations (thanks to our abundant technological props, which make up for areas we are lacking). Yet truth be told, we're actually pretty fragile animals. Our teeth and claws are pitiful. It takes our young forever to mature. We can't climb, run, or swim very fast. To make matters worse, we are thin-skinned and relatively hairless (for mammals, anyway), and even if our waistlines are "robust," we don't have the kind of blubber that keeps other mammals warm in frigid conditions. Without the intelligence and creativity to create shelter and clothing, I doubt our frail species would have ever left the global Goldilocks zones of tropical temperatures that are "just right" for naked humans to live year-round. But we didn't let our limitations stop us; quite the opposite, we turned to the natural resources that made up for our inadequacies. Over time, we turned furs into clothing and learned to seek shelter in caves. This technological growth made it possible for us to venture into less hospitable climates. Eventually, our clothing and home-building skills progressed to a level that has allowed our species to live anywhere on the planet, regardless of the hazardous conditions. But even with our countless inventions and innovations, our bodies are still under the same threats that have dogged our ancestors since the dawn of time. Without the vital necessity that we call shelter, the cold, wind, water, and heat can all take their toll on the human form. Below are some conditions that present the most threat to our bodies.

Hypothermia

Hypothermia is a medical condition in which the environment steals away our body heat faster than our body can produce its own heat to rewarm itself, and this condition is often our greatest threat in the outdoors. The direct translation of this medical term is from the Greek words *hypo* (under) and *thermia* (heat), which we interpret as "low temperature." Normal human body temperature is somewhere around 98.6 degrees Fahrenheit (it can vary in certain individuals), but when that core temperature drops to 95 degrees or lower, any of us would be considered hypothermic, officially. Hypothermia can be caused by cold air, getting wet, windy conditions, or all of these together. Exhaustion, age, body weight, drug use, prescription medicine, alcohol, medical conditions (like hypothyroidism), and other factors can increase a person's risk of hypothermia. To treat it, there are various forms of "rewarming." Passive rewarming is used for mild cases, and it involves supporting the body as it naturally rewarms itself. Dry clothing, blankets, sips of a warm beverage, and calorie-rich foods can all help. Active rewarming is used in more serious cases, and it involves the use of warming items against the trunk first and later to the extremities.

Heating pads and warm, forced air are often used in hospitals, along with careful monitoring for heart issues and shock.

There are three main stages to hypothermia:

First stage: Mild hypothermia victims start with mild shivering, which can progress to violent shivering (sometimes so extreme that the victim cannot strike a match to light a fire or zip up a sleeping bag). This shivering is the body's attempt to generate heat through fast twitch muscle contractions, but this typically does little to raise the body temperature. The reduced circulation of stage one can also manifest as ice-cold extremities, which are the result of the body rerouting blood to keep the head and core warm.

Second stage: Eventually the shivering stops if the victim's body temperature continues to drop. This starts to affect the heart, brain, and other organs and can be classified as moderate hypothermia. The victim may have a slow or weak pulse. Their breathing is also likely to be slower. As their cooling brain begins to affect their performance and behavior, it's common to see clumsiness, irritability, slurred speech, confusion, and tiredness. Many victims have reported that the idea of lying down and "taking a nap" seemed like a great idea at the time.

Third stage: This is also called severe hypothermia, and it can get weird. The victim may barely show respiration and pulse (thirty to forty beats per minute is common in victims with body temperature in the low 80s Fahrenheit). Victims may also have one last surge of energy, with which they perform some strange acts. In 20 to 50 percent of hypothermia deaths, victims remove clothing (it's called paradoxical undressing), and this only worsens their situation. The victim may also bury themselves in snow, soil, sand, or vegetation. Known as terminal burrowing or "hide-and-die syndrome," it's likely to be some autonomous process of the brain stem, creating a primitive burrowing behavior as a last-ditch attempt for protection. Weird, right?

Fight These Heat Loss Mechanisms

In cold weather exposure, these are the four culprits behind heat loss and the resulting condition of hypothermia:

Radiation: This is often our main form of heat loss. When the air is much colder than our body temperature, the heat radiates away from us to be absorbed by the cold air.

Convection: Even when the wind feels still, convection still steals our body heat. This is the process of losing heat to the air or water molecules that move across the skin. The faster the wind is moving, the faster the wind removes your body heat. And if it's raining on you or you fall into cold water, you've got major problems!

Conduction: When we're still and touching something cold (like lying on the frozen ground), we're losing heat through conduction. Never sit or lay on the bare ground without some insulation to block conduction.

Evaporation: It takes heat to turn liquid water into water vapor. As cold wet clothing dries out, the moisture in the clothing will stay cold due to evaporative cooling. We see this when our sweaty or damp clothing dries in the wind, making us feel even colder.

Be Gentle with Hypothermia

CPR may be necessary to keep a severe hypothermia victim alive, but be careful with that chilly heart. Striking the chest of a hypothermia victim (or dropping them during transport) can

(continued next page)

cause a dangerous cardiac arrhythmia (irregular heartbeat). Even a gentle rewarming can induce this potentially fatal heart condition, so don't go making it worse by beating your fists on their chest and screaming "Live!" as if you're on some kind of soap opera. Various arrhythmias are quite common during accidental hypothermia rewarming, and this is why you need to get your hypothermia victim to a hospital, rather than trying your DIY remedies. And don't even consider dunking your hypothermia victim in a hot tub or shoving them into a sauna; you'll send your patient into shock with such aggressive tactics.

Hyperthermia

On the opposite side of the exposure spectrum, we have hyperthermia. This can be translated from the Greek as "high temperature" and can manifest as several different medical conditions. Hyperthermia cannot be compared to having a fever (the body elevating its own temperature, usually to fight off a virus or bacterial infection). Hyperthermia is a higher-than-normal body temperature due to the inability of the body's heat-regulating mechanisms to cope with a high heat environment (like a burning hot desert with no shade). Forms of hyperthermia include heat fatigue, heat syncope (dizziness after lengthy heat exposure), heat cramps, heat exhaustion, and heatstroke—the last two being the worst of the bunch.

Heat Exhaustion: Heat exhaustion can begin when a person's body core temperature starts to go over 100 degrees Fahrenheit. This commonly happens in air temperatures higher than 100 Fahrenheit, but it can happen a little below that when high humidity is present. It's easy for heat exhaustion to occur when a person is exerting themselves heavily in hot conditions, and it's aggravated by a lack of hydration and certain medical problems. When symptoms such as dizziness and fatigue coincide with heavy sweating and clammy skin, it's time to get out of the heat and recover. Lie down—ideally in the shade—elevate both feet, and take plenty of cool drinks until you feel completely better. If a potential heat exhaustion victim is elderly or has medical issues, call 911 if that is an option. Make sure you stay alert to this threat in hot weather and catch heat exhaustion before it turns into heatstroke.

Heatstroke: While most hyperthermia issues are not that dangerous in a healthy adult who can remove themselves from the hot environment, heatstroke is another matter. This form of hyperthermia can kill, and it can do that with surprising speed. When a person transitions from heat exhaustion to heatstroke, their body temperature is usually at or above 104 degrees Fahrenheit, and they will typically have stopped sweating. The victim may also suffer from confusion and dizziness, which may be accompanied by a headache or even a loss of consciousness. From all these symptoms, their hot, dry skin is the easiest to notice. In conditions hot enough for a heatstroke, everyone else will be sweating except for the person having a heatstroke. In everyday conditions, call 911 immediately if someone went from being sweaty to having hot, dry skin. In a survival setting, you may have to treat them yourself. Get your patient out of the sun and have them lie down in the coolest place available. Raise their head (which is opposite from the foot elevation you'd do in heat exhaustion cases). Use a cool, wet cloth or clothing around their body (especially armpits, groin, and neck), and fan them to lower their temperature. If you have chemical "ice" packs in your first aid kit, you can use these for additional cooling. These single use-pouches create an endothermic reaction when you pop the inner packet and the chemicals mix. Work as best as you can to lower this temperature quickly, since body temperatures over 105 degrees Fahrenheit can cause brain damage and a host of other major medical complications. However you do it, once your patient's temperature gets below 104 degrees Fahrenheit, switch out the wet fabric with light dry fabric, and monitor for signs of shock. Get your patient to medical care ASAP, or lead first responders back to the victim.

Other Exposure Risks

The dangers of hypothermia and hyperthermia aren't the only threats you'll face in emergency situations. A ragtag assortment of heat and cold-related injuries can accompany hypothermia or hyperthermia or be present as standalone "injuries" or create their own unique combination of suffering.

Chilblains: This cold exposure condition occurs when the victim has repeated skin exposure in air that is just above freezing. Chilblains will occur with repeated damage to small blood vessels in the skin, and unfortunately, it's long-lasting damage. The itchy red skin discomfort will return after each additional cold exposure. This skin malady frequently affects a person's cheeks, nose, ears, and digits.

Frostbite: Plain and simple, frostbite occurs when a person's tissues actually freeze, destroying those tissues. The loss of toes and ears are common after severe cases, though any exposed skin or extremity can be injured in this way.

Frostnip: Less harsh than frostbite, frostnip is a superficial tissue injury without the deep cellular destruction of frostbite. It's more like a mild burn, and it's common on cheeks, nose tips, ear lobes, and other exposed skin. Wind chill can also play a major role in both frostbite and frostnip. The higher the wind speed, the faster these conditions progress in sub-freezing conditions.

Immersion foot: Also called trench foot, this tissue damage is caused by prolonged or repetitive exposure to cold water (but above freezing temperatures). Being unable to change out wet boots and socks during a cold weather emergency would cause this. The skin of the feet becomes shriveled, pale, and suffers circulatory damage.

Sunburn: Probably our most familiar outdoor injury, sunburn is essentially radiation damage from the UV rays of the sun. It feels a lot like a thermal burn once the damage is manifested, but it takes several hours for the damage to your skin cells and your DNA to show up. When a person doesn't wear UV blocking sunglasses in sunny snowy conditions, the sunburn can even occur in their eyes. Known as "snow blindness," this painful yet temporary condition can blind a person for roughly twenty-four hours (until the eyes naturally heal themselves).

Dehydration: While this is a little different from the other hazards, it's still on the list. Hot, dry winds and other atmospheric conditions can dry out our bodies (particularly our skin, nasal passages, and mouth), leaving us more vulnerable to dehydration. This may not seem like a shelter-related issue, but when a shelter can prevent additional water loss in an arid climate, it becomes a big deal.

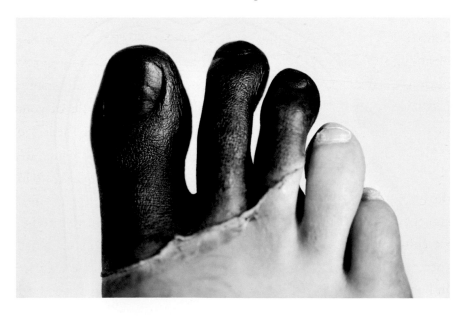

Don't Double Your Frostbite Exposure

In an emergency setting without proper shelter, never thaw out a frostbitten body part if there is a chance it will refreeze. Firstly, it's going to hurt a lot when the damaged tissue thaws out. Secondly, and more importantly, you could do double damage to that tissue when the part freezes again. So if your toes are frozen inside your boots but you still have to hike twenty more miles to get rescued, wait until you reach professional medical care to thaw out. They can pretreat for pain (it's going to be agonizing as your flesh thaws and the nerves begin to inform you of all the damage). Hospital caregivers can also rewarm your tissues gently and in a controlled way. (What were you going to do, roast your feet over the campfire?)

Defend against Scary Things

Sometimes our shelter isn't protecting us from an icy wind or the blistering sun. Sometimes it's defending us from threats that aren't so obvious or predictable. For one simple example, consider your shelter needs in areas with venomous animals. The thin nylon walls of your tent might not seem like much protection, and they wouldn't be if you were facing a bear attack. However, that lightweight layer of nylon fabric might be the thing standing between you and a lethal snakebite in the middle of the night. (Some deadly snakes are attracted to warmth and they like to slither into occupied sleeping bags when the nights get chilly.) How about another example? For thousands of years our ancestors have used rock overhangs as shelter to get out of the weather and create a defendable encampment against opposing tribes and dangerous animals. Today, this same rock overhang on a mountainside could protect us from falling rocks that might randomly tumble down the mountain and roll through our camp while we sleep. Want another example? That abandoned cabin you found in the mountains may look like a film set for a slasher movie, but in reality, the thick doors and walls (and the small windows) are enough to protect you from the grizzly bear attack that a nylon tent could never withstand.

At the end of it all, shelter is about more than just getting away from the heat and cold or hiding from the wind and rain. A shelter might protect you from the weather, creepy crawlies, dangerous animals, and even some of the bad guys. That's right, two-legged predators can be a threat. In such very rare situations, the right shelter may hide you from unfriendly eyes thanks to its placement or camouflage.

However you look at it and whatever the situation, survival shelters are about protection from harm, in all its different forms.

Double Your Defenses

In general, the elements are your worst foe. Yet in the occasional and odd situation, a bad person or predatory animal could pose a real threat to your safety. I hate to burst your bubble, but the cost of the tranquility of nature is a very real vulnerability. Away from other people and removed from law enforcement, you'll need to provide your own security. That's why I recommend bringing a friend to all possible outdoor excursions. You have to sleep sometime, and with the "buddy system" in place, you can take turns watching in the night if anything seems "wrong" out there. This second set of eyes and ears can double your defensive capabilities and make any shelter more secure.

2

The Shelters You Bring

By the end of this book, you'll have a lot of options to consider for emergency shelter construction, and any one of these "made from scratch" shelter styles might just save your life in an emergency. But why start out empty-handed? Why struggle to make something the hard way, when you can simply plan ahead and bring what you need? In this chapter, we'll look at your most foundational shelter against the elements: the clothing you wear. Your decisions on clothing and outerwear may not seem like a big deal when you set out for a hike on a nice afternoon, but a person's choice of clothing is often the first place that things start going right (or wrong) in a survival situation. Furthermore, we'll look at a variety of portable shelters that you should bring with you on every trip into the wild. We'll even explore some shelter options for emergencies that don't happen in the wilderness. For years, preparedness enthusiasts have been saying, "It's better to have it and not need it, than to need it and not have it." I couldn't agree more, and this definitely needs to be your mantra when preparing for the unexpected.

Your mom has been telling you to bring a jacket or sweater along with you since you were a little child. Maybe now you'll pay attention to her (and to me). Dress according to the worst or most extreme weather that the season may throw at you. Stuff your pockets, backpack, and vehicle with smart shelter options for everyday predicaments and emergency situations. You can even plan ahead for the others in your party, like the ones who weren't smart enough to do so. Shelter begins with the clothes on your back.

Clothing

Dress for the conditions. It's simple advice, but picking the right garments for an outdoor excursion can be a really important decision. Our clothing is, in essence, a mobile shelter that protects us against the weather and the environment. I'm no fashion influencer, and I worry more about function than form, but I do take the time to focus on fabrics when buying outdoor clothing and deciding what to wear for an outing. Many people wear all the wrong types of clothing (like cotton jeans and T-shirts) during outdoor activities, so how do we get it right?

Defend against the Cold

Our cold weather clothing choices are obvious and important decisions. With maladies like hypothermia and frostbite just waiting around the corner for anyone who ventures out underdressed, our threats are readily apparent. However, this doesn't mean that our clothing choices are so apparent. Here are some of the options for fighting the cold.

- Build a Base Layer: In the old days, outdoors people wore scratchy wool "long johns" and were glad to have them when things turned chilly. Today, we can find softer versions of these wool undergarments, and we can take advantage of modern synthetic fabric sewn into patterns for long underwear products. Whichever fabric you pick, you'll want to have long sleeves, and a two-piece design will allow you to go to the bathroom much easier.

- Add a Mid Layer: Wool can continue to come in handy in the form of pants, shirts, and sweaters. A synthetic hooded sweatshirt could also offer a lot of warmth and comfort in the cold.

- Finish With an Outer Layer: Various coats, jackets, and parkas can finish your outfit, as well as insulated "snow pants." When possible, choose well-insulated coats with hoods, and lean toward synthetic insulation if the conditions might turn wet. For "guaranteed" dry conditions, down insulation (made from tiny bird feathers) is suitable, warm, and very lightweight. When possible, choose outerwear that has a waterproof shell like Gore-Tex or some similar waterproof yet breathable fabric. Don't Forget the Accessories: Gloves, hats, scarves, ski masks, balaclavas, and many other insulated accessories can round out your gear list. You'll also want to have insulated boots and thick socks (ideally, wool or synthetic, not cotton). For the perpetual deep freeze, you may even want to consider buying boots that are a size bigger than your normal boots. These allow enough room to wear two pairs of socks at once. UV protecting sunglasses or goggles can also be important when dealing with sun and snow together.

Cotton Kills!

I know I'll get some hate mail from the Cotton Growers Council, but hear me out. Cotton fabric is an amazingly durable and comfortable material, and folks have been

(continued next page)

making everything from pajamas to work pants from this remarkable fiber for a very long time. Here's the problem, though; cotton fiber is great at holding water, and it can retain this fluid (and others) for quite some time. If you remember our heat loss mechanisms from "Chapter One: Understand the Threats," wet clothing can conduct away body heat and can also lead to evaporative cooling as the fabric dries out. When we have wet cotton clothing against our skin, it naturally cools us down. This is a great feature in a hot desert climate during the sweltering daytime high temperatures, but it's dangerous in other conditions. When you're experiencing cold weather and your cotton clothing gets wet, you'll end up even colder (and start heading toward hypothermia). We've all probably worn wet blue jeans that didn't dry out for hours, and this is my point against cotton clothing for cold or variable weather. This type of cloth holds moisture too long and conducts away body heat. One of the worst offenders is a set of cotton long johns, which numerous garment brands sell. These are great to wear around the house, but they are a perilous choice for a base layer under your outdoor clothing. If it's cold enough for long underwear, it's cold enough for hypothermia—and that's not the kind of weather to wear cotton.

Adjust for Variable Weather

Garment options for "nice weather" can be just as important as your clothing choices for the extremes of heat and cold. In spring and autumn, the weather can change quickly, and we need to be able to modify our garments to match. Get ready for a hot afternoon or a cold snap with these versatile choices.

- Start with a Base: Synthetic fabric underwear and socks can be your base layer for moderate or changing conditions.
- Meet in the Middle: Wearing mid-weight wool or synthetic pants can be a great choice for mid-range weather, as these aren't so thick that they will roast you if the day turns hot, but they do offer some protection from cold and minor injury (thorn scratches and such). A mid-weight long-sleeved shirt can be opened to cool you down or buttoned up for warmth. A synthetic T-shirt or light-weight undershirt can also allow you to take off the long-sleeved shirt, if needed.
- Remember Your Jacket: Mom was right; bring a jacket! This could be any kind of jacket that suits the terrain and season, but a packable waterproof jacket can offer a little warmth and a lot of rain protection in a compact form. Failing that, bring something else that can pass for rain gear (like a poncho), should things turn wet.
- Enjoy the Extras: Protect your feet with hiking boots and synthetic socks. Protect your hands with a pair of lightweight work gloves. Bring a hat, as well, for sun protection and a little extra warmth.

Dress for the Heat

Using clothing choices to try to stay cool is a lot harder than using smart garment options to warm up. You can always add more clothing to warm up, but it's hard to add or change clothing to cool down. Still, there are some smart choices for hot weather clothing, and we'll explore them now.

- Don't Go Commando: Synthetic fabric underwear can be your base layer in hot, humid weather or hot, dry weather, as these can double for swimwear. I know you may want to skip this layer in very hot weather, but you may be sorry for it. You're already suffering from the heat, you don't need to add chaffing to your list of troubles

- Keep Your Mid-Layer Covered: Despite the heat and your desire to shed clothing, it's important to keep your skin covered to block the heat and UV rays of the sun. Select thin fabric, a loose fit, and light colors for synthetic pants and shirts. Long sleeves are still preferable, and zip-off pant legs (turning the pants into shorts) are nice. You'll want your clothing to breathe while keeping as much skin covered as possible.

- Add an Option: You won't normally think of outerwear for hot climates, but rain gear is the one exception. This could be a "pants and jacket" rain set or something looser (like a poncho).

- Bring the Extras: Lightweight boots or "hiking shoes" with thin synthetic socks will provide protection without a lot of weight. Wearing a very thin liner sock underneath your normal socks will also help with moisture control and help to diminish blistering. Don't forget your sunglasses, a wide thin hat to block the sun, and some very thin work gloves.

Boil Away Your Fungus

There is a place where cotton fabric makes sense (outside of the daytime desert scenario). In jungles, tropical regions, or any other hot and humid climate, cotton does have an advantage over synthetic clothing for garments like socks

(continued next page)

and underwear. Fungal skin infections can spread through dirty clothing, but cotton clothing can be periodically boiled and then dried over the fire to kill the fungal organisms without significant shrinkage of said garment. Try that with wool socks or synthetic underwear and they'll shrink down to doll clothing size.

Survival Shelters

Even the best outdoor clothing is no substitute for a sheltering structure to protect you from the elements. If there's no guarantee of finding a cabin or cave along your path (and you shouldn't count on that), carrying some kind of portable shelter is the next best thing. Whether you're a prepper stocking a "bug-out bag" for doomsday, or you're a hiker just looking to make a few miles on the trail, it's never a bad idea to carry your own shelter assets. From affordable supplies like trash bags and space blankets to ultralight backpacking tents and high-end sleeping bags, this gear can provide you with a home away from home and give you great protection from the elements. Don't let your budget prevent you from finding the right shelter necessities to carry into the wild or to stock for emergencies. You never know when they will come in handy.

Space Blankets

You won't last long in harsh weather, especially if you're caught without the right clothing. And since shelter will always be one of your top survival priorities, a simple space blanket can be one of the cheapest shelter supplies you can buy. So why is it called a "space" blanket? These lightweight blankets were developed by NASA's Marshall Space Flight Center in 1964 for the US space program. They are

commonly made from a thin sheet of plastic, which is coated with a metallic gold or silver layer. Under ideal conditions, this reflective coating can bounce back up to 97 percent of radiated heat. And here's the best part, in today's flooded survival market, space blankets are very cheap and readily available. These are available as flat sheets that can be wrapped around someone to reflect their body heat back toward that person. The same reflective material is also used to create something like a sleeping bag, which offers better coverage and performs better in high wind (the flat sheet version tends to flap in the breeze). There's no excuse for skimping out on this survival resource, even if you're broke. Space blankets can cost as little as one dollar each. Do keep in mind that you get what you pay for. Thick and larger space blankets may cost something like five dollars each, though they are much more durable. In any case, even the "fancy" ones are still cheap enough that you could carry several in your outdoor kit or vehicle. Nothing else this small and lightweight can offer this much protection.

The Space Heat Continuum

Space blankets work great—when they are able to bounce heat back to a human body that is radiating heat—but what happens when there is no heat to reflect? When someone is suffering from hypothermia, their cold body is radiating off very little heat. With little heat to reflect, the blanket may feel like it's not even working at all. The trick to using these blankets correctly is to use them early in a cold exposure scenario. Shroud yourself in this shiny wrapper while you're still radiating plenty of heat, and you'll stay warmer through the ordeal. Once all of your skin is ice cold, it's too late for the space blanket to help on its own. You'd need an extra heat source inside the blanket to rewarm a very cold person (something like a hot water bottle).

Ponchos

Ponchos are "throw over" rain gear that come in a diverse assortment of sizes, colors, and materials. Some are as cheap as space blankets and made from thin, clear (or colored) plastic sheeting. With these, you definitely get what you pay for, as the dollar ponchos are often thinner plastic than a trash bag. Heavier ponchos may be constructed from vinyl or nylon, which will hold up better against wear and tear. Military-style ponchos can even be purchased with an insulating liner that adds warmth to the normal wind and rain protection they can offer. Obviously, it's better to spend a little bit more on your poncho

to get one with greater durability, but any poncho is better than none. Acting like a mobile tent, the large surface area of a poncho offers rain protection while walking or standing, and it can even cover your backpack, too. Ponchos can be stretched out on the ground as a barrier to block moisture, or pitched as a tarp shelter. Clear plastic ponchos can even double as the covering for a solar still (a simple contraption that makes water from steam inside a pit in the ground, using the greenhouse effect created by the clear plastic covering). There's also a side benefit to carrying brightly colored ponchos. These can act as emergency signal flags, particularly when attached to a long pole and waved like a flag. There are documented search and rescue "saves" that are attributed to lost hikers waving colorful ponchos like a rescue signal flag to catch the eye of searchers in aircraft. As a final benefit, there's something to be said for the value of a camouflaged or earth tone poncho. When considering stealth as a survival strategy, you may not want to wear a giant orange plastic one. Whatever quality you choose to buy and whatever color it may be, ponchos are multiuse wearable shelters that are too cheap and too lightweight to ignore. In fact, it wouldn't be bad to have all the colors mentioned here—clear plastic, bright orange, and something camouflaged.

Bivy Sacks

Most people (and even a number of outdoors-people) are unfamiliar with the word and concept of a bivy sack. The word bivy is actually short for the word *bivouac*, which means to camp somewhere. There are ties to both the military and mountain climbers, as both groups may occasionally need a lightweight and highly mobile shelter system. Often structured like sleeping bag covers or tiny tubular tents, there is no shortage of bivy sacks on the market. Some of these shelters are intended to replace a sleeping bag in emergencies and lined with reflective space blanket material. Other bivys are crafted from waterproof material and are intended to be used as sleeping bag covers. While these products lack the warmth and softness of a traditional sleeping bag, they can be a great addition to survival kits due to their small size and light weight.

Don't Ignore Trash Bags

For just a few dollars, you can purchase a box of huge trash bags and use them for all kinds of shelter purposes. Giant "drum liner" bags are meant to fit into fifty-five-gallon barrels as trash bags. These are usually thicker and stronger plastic than the next toughest bag, and these are large

(continued next page)

enough to act as a bivy sack for a smaller person. You can also transform a large trash bag into a crude poncho by tearing a hole in the bottom corner and wearing it pulled down over your entire body. As another common shelter element, I often turn big trash bags into a ground cloth material to go under tents and other shelters. By cutting the bag open on the side and bottom, it can become a larger piece of plastic (like a tarp). You can even incorporate this DIY tarp material into your shelter roof for better rain protection. Your creativity is the only limit with this versatile plastic product. And once you divide the cost of a box of trash bags by the number of bags, you end up with shelter items that cost less than a dollar apiece.

Tents and Sleeping Bags

Tents and sleeping bags offer a taste of home comfort in the wild places of the earth, and there's no shortage of makes and models to consider.

Pick a Tent

Since this is your "home away from home," you'll want to make sure it's a good fit for your prospective needs. If you're planning to go camping often, using the tent throughout the seasons and years, something durable is a great choice. Read the reviews, talk to the folks at the camping store, and ask your outdoorsy friends. Many of the name brands that have been around for years will provide you with a fine tent. And if you're only concerned with emergency preparedness, you'll still want a rugged tent that can hold up to heavy use and bad weather. When it comes to your portable home, don't skimp on the cost.

Add a Sleeping Bag and Pad

You'll freeze to death lying in an empty tent in cold weather without a sleeping bag around you and a pad underneath you. Your tent isn't the only part of your home on the go. You'll need something that can pass for a mattress and bedding. I used to be a big fan of sleeping pads that held air and had a foam core, yet packed down small for carrying, but I've grown tired of them eventually springing air leaks and deflating in the night. That's why I've switched over to simple roll-up foam pads—much thicker and lighter than yoga mats, these pads are bulky, but they are warm and tough. Similarly, your sleeping bag should be warm and tough to match. I tend toward synthetic fill mummy bags, but there are plenty of fillings and shapes on the market. Just keep in mind that the degree rating on the bag is more of a "survival" rating than a comfort ration. That "zero degree" bag may keep you alive at 0 degrees Fahrenheit, but you won't be warm; it will be great at 15 or 20 degrees Fahrenheit and probably too hot to use above 40 degrees

Fahrenheit. Just add twenty degrees to the listed rating and then you'll know it's right.

Shop for Used Camping Gear

It might be someone's trash, or it might be a discounted treasure. When outdoor enthusiasts replace or upgrade their gear, they might make room for it by getting rid of the old one. Of course, it's all going to come down to luck and persistence, but it's possible to find lightweight backpacking tents and sleeping bags—used but in good condition (and at a great price). Check your local sales websites or meet people at old fashioned yard sales and swap meets. Focus on name-brand gear (like Kelty, North Face, and Mountain Hardwear) and newer models when looking at used gear. Things that still have their packaging can be a good sign, too. Don't let somebody push their trash off on you. That old moldy canvas army tent will probably split in half at the first good gust of wind. If you're shopping for tents, insist to see them fully set up. By doing this, you'll be able to check that each tent pole is present and the tent is in good condition. Check every single zipper, button, and accessory, too, before you fork over your hard-earned cash. And if you get a piece of gear with an odd smell, add some distilled vinegar to the wash to neutralize the odor. In cases where gear is more "personal," like sleeping bags, you could also use a sanitizing laundry product that is not chlorine-based. Just make sure you don't use pure bleach on the fabric; undiluted bleach is very corrosive to nylon and other common camping gear fabrics, including those commonly used for sleeping bags.

Vehicle Supplies

Your vehicle is like a rolling storehouse. Even a small car can transport much more weight than you could carry on your back, and unless somebody breaks a window, this gear is protected from the weather. As you consider what kind of shelter supplies you might want to stock in your backpack or survival kit, I'd encourage you to also consider the shelter supplies in your car. We'll discuss the merits (and drawbacks) of using a vehicle as a shelter in Chapter Eight, "Shelter in Modern Emergencies," but for now, let's think about the supplies that vehicle can carry.

Extra Clothing: Whether you commute a long way to work or you travel a lot or you just use the car to go to the grocery store and back again, you'll want to stock some extra clothing and shelter supplies in that vehicle. Your typical business attire may look great in the office, and it's what you'll be wearing as you commute back and forth, but this is unlikely to be the right wardrobe for a crisis. Most business clothing is not well suited for warmth or traveling through the outdoors, and you won't get much fighting, running, or bushwhacking done in high heels. You'll also want this clothing to reflect the current season and the most extreme weather that the season might deliver. If you don't swap out the clothing to match the environment, you'll find out the hard way that your extra shorts and flip flops are fairly useless in a midwinter blizzard. Choose comfortable garments that will serve your needs, including footwear that can keep you going for miles (on the road or off it). Naturally, you'll swap out your clothes each season, and you'll want to keep up with any weight loss or gain you might experience. This preparedness can be done for free, if you take advantage of clothing you already own.

Items for Warmth: In addition to a change of clothes and footwear, you'll also want to consider items for warmth when you are stuck inside the vehicle (or somewhere without these resources). You'll need to be carrying enough "warmth items" to cover your maximum number of passengers. For example, if your vehicle can carry five passengers and a driver, you'll need six items for warmth. These can be sleeping bags (though that gets expensive), blankets (a cheaper option, though not as warm), space blankets (cheap but chilly), as well as coats, hats, gloves, and related items.

3

The Shelters You Find

It's hard to imagine the gritty reality of our ancient past from the perspective of a spoiled modern human in present times, but there was an age before we had even dreamt of little mud. It was a time in the distant past, and a very alien world compared to our material-driven cultures today. Long before our ancestors developed the skills to make complex tools like axes or learned to build their own homes from raw materials sourced in nature, they sought out the natural shelters that were a part of the landscape. So different from us, yet so alike—they just wanted a place to call "home," as we all do. We can see this drive to find shelter in the abundant archeological finds in caves and under rock overhangs around the world, dating back to the earliest part of the Stone Age. Jump forward to our time, and we can still find these shelters in the wild terrain of the wilderness and the everyday stomping grounds of our local parks and forests. From the protection offered by land features and vegetation, to cozy little caves and hollow trees, the environment can occasionally provide structures that offer a haven from the elements and a place to warm up when we are cold. We simply have to train our eyes to look for them and understand the risks in using them. Remember that "the only free cheese is on the trap," and these ready-made accommodations can come with a few drawbacks (namely, animal inhabitants who also think of these structures as "home"). In this chapter, we'll look at the shelters you find in the wild, such as caves, rock overhangs, hollow trees, land formations, and various vegetative cover.

Land Formations

Finding protection isn't always a brutal struggle or a DIY project that takes hours of hard labor. Sometimes, the very terrain itself can offer us some protection from the wind and other weather conditions. From protected low spots to mountains that block the storms, being in the right place at the right time can make all the difference.

Low Areas

One simple way to get out of the elements is to drop down to a lower area. Since hilltops and ridges get hit with more wind, which can create dangerous wind chill temperatures in colder seasons and areas, the protection of valleys, ravines, canyons, and depressions can be a welcome relief. Valleys are often large low-lying areas between large landforms like mountains and ridges. These spots have protection to offer, though they can be colder in the late hours of the night as the coldest air falls to the bottom of the valley before morning. Smaller and more protected canyons and gorges are typically deep ravines between cliffs or steep embankments. These often contain areas where most of the wind is blocked, but they are susceptible to flooding. Similarly, depressions of all kinds can provide a place to seek refuge. It may be something small like a ditch or pit, or something much larger. These low areas are fine for a few hours of temporary shelter, but due to their flooding risk, they aren't usually a great choice for a shelter building site.

High Areas

Mountains, hills, dunes, and cliffs can all provide shelter, when we are able to get on the side that is out of the driving rain and howling wind. There will always be a windward side and a leeward side to raised landforms. The windward side is the area that is struck by the prevailing wind and storms. It's usually the wetter side, too, since mountains and ridges tend to "squeeze" the moisture out of the clouds as the weather tries to pass over. The leeward side of a landform is typically the drier side, as it is protected from the prevailing wind by the landform, which can be a large or small body. Obviously, mountains can block a lot of weather, as can ridges (a chain of mountains with an elevated crest that runs for some distance). Buttes are like small mountains or large hills, which are often isolated and have a flat top with steep sides. Cliffs can be part of many different landforms, presenting a vertical or very steep rock face of significant height. Any of these can provide some relief from storms, and they can often provide us with more protected areas to build structures of our own.

Thickets and Brush

We shouldn't emulate everything that the animals do, but there's some wisdom in the way that animals take advantage of natural vegetative cover. Whether hiding from predators or simply getting out of the rain, many animals head for thickets and brushy areas to protect themselves. I'm not suggesting that you crawl into a briar patch like a rabbit, but by taking shelter in brush and thick vegetation, the wind is blocked and you can take advantage of a microclimate. Evergreen vegetation can offer a wind block in the winter months, and tree canopy can provide relief from the burning summer sun. And when you're ready to build a camp (rather than just hide in the bushes), setting up a camp on the leeward side of brushy areas can really take the edge out of icy winds.

Evergreen Trees

This is another instinctive place to get out of the storms and shield yourself from bad weather. Hiding under an evergreen tree can offer partial protection from precipitation, especially snowfall. And when the lower branches hang down to the ground, they can even block some of the wind. The two biggest factors in the usefulness of an evergreen tree as a shelter are the density of the foliage and the shape of the tree. When the needles or leaves are thin, the precipitation can fall right through, but when they are thick, they can interrupt the path of the precipitation and often redirect it toward the edges of the tree. This is called the drip line, and it represents the perimeter of the tree's foliage. Additionally, when the shape of the tree makes a natural conical roof, it's a much better shelter than a tree that is shaped more like an umbrella.

Watch Out for the Bugs

I've walked through some dense areas of ticks, but the worst I ever encountered was a tick nursery under a huge sheltering cedar tree. We were hiking around looking for medicinal plants and wanted to check out this tree that looked like a natural shelter. The branches hung to the ground all around it and the needles were thick. It was a great place to seek protection, and apparently some mother ticks thought

(continued next page)

the same thing. Within just a few minutes, our group had picked up hundreds of tiny tick larvae. No bigger than a flake of crushed black pepper, these micro marauders are attracted to anything warm and moving—they're keen to suck your blood so that they can grow out of their larval form and into the next stage of life. Be aware that a good shelter for you can also mean a good shelter for parasites and other creatures.

Hollow Trees

North America has a long tradition of creative people using tree hollows, both standing and fallen, as shelter. Certainly, the First Nations of the continent took advantage of hollow trees and logs in the massive old growth forests of the Eastern Woodlands. When the colonists came later, they took advantage of these tree cavities, as well. The eighteenth-century history of the Virginia Colony contains one of the earliest references to a family living in a hollow tree. In 1744, Joseph Hampton and his two sons lived for most of the year in a hollow sycamore located in the Shenandoah Valley (now known as Clarke County, Virginia). A few years later, the French explorer "Father Bonnecamp" described a huge cottonwood tree on the bank of the Ohio River which was so huge, twenty-nine men could sit beside each other—inside the tree. Later still, Thomas Spencer Sharpe became one of the first Caucasian settlers to grow crops in Tennessee. He spent the winter of 1778 living inside a giant hollow sycamore. Today, huge hollow trees are scarce in North America, but there are still plenty of small hollow trees and logs that can provide temporary shelter from the elements.

And now for the bad news: taking a page from the history books is not risk-free. Places that offer shelter, offer it to more than just

humans. You may find a spot that looks like a perfectly good shelter, but upon further inspection, it contains venomous animals (like spiders and snakes) or it contains years of bat guano (which can transmit disease). Inviting shelters are seldom unoccupied in the wild, so weigh the risks before claiming the rewards. If I need to get out of the freezing rain and howling wind, I'll take my chances in a tree hollow with the snakes, spiders, bats, and excrement. If other options make more sense, I'll explore those instead.

Family Saved by Hollow Tree

Stories of people living in hollow trees and logs are more than just distant historical facts. Over the winter of 2012, a family of three spent six days sheltering in a vacant hollow tree in an old-growth Oregon forest. Their ordeal began on Sunday, January 29, when the mother, father, and adult son went looking for hedgehog mushrooms. These valuable fungi fetch a high price at fancy restaurants, but their quest nearly cost the family their lives. Like a fairytale gone wrong, the mushroom hunters got lost and spent a very cold, rough week sheltered in the hollow tree. The cold rains prevented them from building a fire for warmth or as a signal. Heavy vegetation prevented search and rescue efforts, by ground and by air. By the end of their predicament, the cold wet conditions had given family members frostbite and hypothermia, and one of them had gotten injured, but the sheltering tree cavity had kept them alive long enough to finally be spotted by a search helicopter in one of the few forest clearings.

Study Your Species

Not every tree species can rot out in the center and leave an intact outer husk big enough to provide shelter. Some trees don't reach a large enough size, while others have wood that is resistant to rotting. In the Eastern and Central

(continued next page)

United States, sycamore (*Platanus occidentalis*) trees are the most likely to provide sheltering cavities. On the west coast, the mighty redwoods (*Sequoia sempervirens*) and other cedar family members can provide hollow logs on the ground and standing tree cavities. Keep an eye out for these species and learn the others that can provide refuge on the run.

Boulders and Rocky Outcrops

You don't need to find a naturally occurring version of Stonehenge; just a few taller rocks in a cluster will suffice for protection. In some areas, large boulders on the surface of the land may be just the right size and arrangement to offer shelter from the wind and driving rain, not to mention offering shade during the heat of the day. In the Northern Hemisphere, people have long known that the cooler side of a rocky outcrop or boulder is the north side (and conversely, the south side in the Southern Hemisphere). In fact, archeologists in North America have found pits on the north side of boulders where early people preserved meat, likely buried under ice and snow. Of course, the meat was long gone, but the pits and the bones with stone tool cut marks allow us to piece the story together. Furthermore, modern experiments have proven that this technique works surprisingly well. Since the sun wouldn't hit these areas in the colder months, the ice and frozen meat would presumably last much longer. These boulders and outcrops can also create a "micro-climate" when you are able to hide from the wind and bask in the warmth of the sunlight on the south side or burn a fire in these protected spots. Similarly, rocky outcrops can offer protection, and even act as a structural element for dwellings you might construct.

(For example, creating a lean-to against a boulder can get you two walls for the price of one.)

Rock Overhangs

They're not quite caves, but these natural stone shelters seem to call upon our instincts to find cover and protection. Rock overhangs and stone ledges have long been favorite shelters of our ancestors, and they offer more than just a place to get out of the cold rain. Rock overhangs are known by many names. The rock shelter, rockhouse, crepuscular cave, and bluff shelter are just a few of the titles. Whatever they are called in your area, these rocky landforms are shallow openings that form near the base of a cliff or similar form. They can also be eroded areas at the bottom edge of massive stone outcrops or boulders. Some are deep and almost cave-like, while others don't provide enough room to lie down. Formed in different ways from dissolved stone (karst) caves, rock overhangs can occur when a soft rock stratum suffers erosion and weathering underneath a more resistant stratum, undercutting the landform. While water can perform this erosion, wind erosion (Aeolian erosion) is also capable of excavating these areas in dry climates. The cycle of freezing and thawing can also wear down the rock. In areas damp and cold, a process called frost spalling can remove the rock, one tiny flake at a time. As wet porous rock freezes, the frost expansion flakes off little bits of rock, which can then be blown away in the wind or washed away by water. Whichever process forms these undercut rock areas, they can often be used "as is" for shelter or have the opening partially covered for even better fortification.

Overhang Hazards

A "cave in" is the most obvious hazard you'd face when spending any amount of time under a rock ledge, and although the chance of this happening while you're under it is minimal, it's still important to survey the structure before committing to it as your shelter for the night. Look for any loose rock overhead, and look for recently fallen rock on the ground underneath the shelter. It's also likely to be dry under there, so dust may be easily stirred up by moving around in this protected area. This isn't a problem, unless there are pathogens in that dust. Mice and other rodents frequently use these shelters, and in areas with hantavirus and other scary organisms, you probably don't want to be living in that pestilent dust.

Caves

Who wouldn't want to play "caveman" and seek protection in one of our oldest habitations—a cave? We've been using these rocky homes since the Stone Age, and they still have a lot to offer today. Now, I know what the naysayers are thinking: what's so amazing about a cold damp hole in the rock that's probably full of spiders (and bigger threats)? Well, here's why these natural landforms can be a safe haven in an emergency.

- There's a stable temperature in caves. Once you're a few feet underground, the temperature doesn't change much unless you have a strong draft. Depending on the latitude, caves in North America range between 40 and 60 degrees Fahrenheit (being warmer in

the south and cooler up north). So when it's frigid outside of the cave, the interior will actually seem warm by comparison. And who wouldn't want to crawl into a cool dark cave during the heat of a summer day or in the desert? It may be as much as 60 degrees cooler in there!

- There's often plenty of room. Unlike rock overhangs, which are typically small and shallow, many caves can stretch on for miles underground. This gives you all the room you'd need for storage and plenty of area to set up supplementary shelter inside the cave itself. Some anthropologists and archeologists say that "cavemen" built hide or plant-covered tents inside their caves for extra warmth and protection.

- Defend yourself. The cave offers a built-in defensive action. Anything that wants to "get you" has to come through the opening. This becomes a natural choke point, and it's easier to defend than standing in the open.

Cave Safety

There are three main issues that impact our safety when using caves as a shelter: animals, air, and fire. In bat-filled caves, the droppings (guano) can be filled with pathogens and parasites, and it's even flammable (they used to make gun powder with guano, sulfur, and charcoal powder). You may even run into animals bigger than a bat (like a bear)! Just watch out in there, as you'll probably be sharing the cave with other creatures. Secondly, the air quality can be poor, so it's often best to hang out near the entrance, not in the back. Finally, don't try to burn a fire in a cave. It damages a fragile ecosystem with smoke, and it can damage you by expanding the overhead rocks from the rising heat (which can collapse on you).

The Most Dangerous Cave

All caves present hazards to those who'd dare to venture inside, but coastal caves (also known as sea caves) are often the most dangerous. These can be blocked or

(continued next page)

even filled by high tides, sometimes in a matter of minutes. When exploring caves in coastal areas, determine the high tide line in the area and check the interior of the cave for a line of seaweed or driftwood that could mean water comes in there. Sea caves that flood with the tide will usually have a damp smell and stay damp after the tide goes out. Standing water, like rock pools, can also be a sign that the cave floods with the tide. In a bad storm, it's best to avoid sea caves entirely—since the storm surge can push water much higher than the normal high tide lines.

Hot Spots

These are a little weird, as shelters go, but when you can take advantage of them, they are certainly worth considering. Hot spots can be divided into two categories—a solar sink and a geothermal site. The former is an area heated by the sun, and the latter is an area heated from the earth. Here's what you need to know about them both.

Solar Sinks

In desert climates and hot sunny weather, the heat of the sun can be absorbed and stored in rocks and boulders during the daytime and released slowly in the night. In general, these warm rocks won't provide any cover overhead (unless they are solar heated rock overhangs), but they do provide a warm place to lay down on a cold desert night. Plan ahead in order to take full advantage of this natural resource. Find a darker and flatter rock outcropping with full sun exposure all day. Assemble some bedding materials, like dry grass or leaves (to create a softer mattress on the unyielding stone surface). Don't cover the sunbaked stone until the sun goes down, since you want it to absorb as much heat as possible. Keep in mind that these solar sinks might not stay warm all night, but they can give you hours of warmth and allow you to get some quality sleep before the night gets really frigid. I'd also recommend a backup plan for warmth in those frigid pre-dawn hours.

Geothermal Sites

These are a jackpot when you find them in nature, though they can pose some serious risks. Geothermal hotspot sites are common in Yellowstone, the islands of Hawaii, and Iceland. These hotspots are caused by volcanic activity near the surface and may manifest as heated ground or stones, hot surface water, or steam vents from underground. These can provide a warm place to sleep, but they can also release toxic gasses and create burns. Use great caution when experimenting with geothermal sites as a source of warmth and shelter.

Dangers From Below

If you decide to snuggle up for the night next to some smoking vent from the depths of the earth, take caution. Steam coming out of the ground is creepy enough, as if some cauldron in Hell is boiling over. Volcanic gasses are another thing entirely. Carbon dioxide gas is a common emission in volcanic areas, and this gas can reach high concentrations in low-lying areas. Just 3 percent of carbon dioxide in the air can cause headaches, dizziness, rapid pulse, and difficulty breathing. At levels that are over 15 percent carbon dioxide in the air, a person can quickly lose consciousness and

(continued next page)

suffocate to death. Carbon dioxide isn't the only dangerous gas leaking from the ground in volcanic hot spots. Sulfur dioxide, hydrogen sulfide, and hydrogen halides can also be present, all of which can be harmful to human life (and other organisms). If you happen to see dead vegetation and animal bones around any kind of geothermal vent or in a low lying volcanic area, that's a great indicator that the area should be avoided. Don't add your bones to the pile.

4

Tarp Shelters

If we could go back and visit historic times, we would see a wide range of tents, teepees, yurts, and huts build from stick and rope frames, then covered with leather and/or fabric that had been sewn together into a covering. Some of these materials were crude at best, while others were way ahead of their time. One of the best materials was a canvas that had been treated for water repellency using various oils and waxes—which is pretty impressive considering that most of these forebears hadn't figured out indoor plumbing yet. Our ancestors knew that guarding against the elements was absolutely crucial in the outdoors, and without this protection, they were as good as dead. They also knew that their temporary dwelling didn't need to be a palace, it just needed to defend them from the cold and the wet in a way that their clothing could not. And since necessity is the mother of invention, the various climates and materials of the world gave rise to an impressive array of shelters than could be built from tarps or tarp-like materials. Jumping forward to modern times, today we have a

much more diverse assortment of materials than our predecessors had access to—ones that we can convert into lean-tos, teepees, tents, hammocks, and other useful structures; these different shelter shapes can be built using many different things. We can still make use of the old traditional building supplies. We also have plastic tarps, sail materials, parachute cloth, and similar fabric that offer higher performance than canvas. Whichever you choose (or have available), the directions in this chapter will give you the tools to create the right shelter for the right conditions and location you may be facing.

Build in the Right Location

Before you set up the first stick or tie the first knot for any survival shelter, the first thing you'll need to do is determine a suitable location to build. Even if your building skills are legendary, plopping down a magnificent shelter in a terrible location will make it a terrible shelter, and the location choice can even endanger the inhabitants. For example, you may set up a beautiful hut in the bottom of a steep ravine to get out of the wind, but what happens when the rain comes down hard? Water could pool in the shelter, forcing you to abandon it. This means that you wasted your time and energy, and you have no shelter to show for your hard work. Or worse yet, a flash flood could sweep through the ravine and scour away any sign of your existence (including your dead, drowned body). (I know that's a little dramatic, but if it gets the point across, I did my job.) Here are some guidelines to consider when choosing a build location, and please—take them seriously.

- Use natural protection. All those weather-blocking land features, vegetation, and forms that we discussed in Chapter Three, "The Shelters You Find," can block the full force of the weather that is trying to hit your shelter. Choose a building site that takes advantage of natural protection from the weather. When possible, avoid building on open ground, hilltops, or peaks—which will be hit the hardest by foul weather. Just make sure that you avoid areas that include their own hazards. You don't want to build where loose rocks, dead limbs, or entire trees could fall on your camp. The first thing I'll do when considering a spot to build in my native Eastern woodlands is to look up to spot dead branches that may fall on my shelter or injure me.

- Think about water. Skip the low lying areas to avoid flooding, rainfall pooling, or rain running underneath your shelter. This means you should avoid building in ditches, gullies, drainages, and low spots. Instead, choose a slight rise in the surrounding terrain. You'll also want to avoid building near any body of water. There are often more biting insects around water and a significantly higher humidity.

- Check for pests, predators, and other problems with the build site. This is a motley group of hazards and annoyances, including but not limited to poison ivy, nearby beehives, a higher mosquito population, or a territorial scratching posts for predators (like bears and big cats). I like to check the building site for even smaller animals—like ants—by scraping away the vegetation to the bare dirt. If I'm about to be on an anthill, the disturbance will bring them out of their colony. If I see evidence of pests, predators, or troublemakers, I'll pick a different build site.

- Be fire friendly. You'll want any fire pits or cooking hearths to be at least twelve feet (four meters) away from your shelter and on the leeward side of your structure (downwind of your hut). This is particularly important when building with dry leaves, grasses, pine needles, and other flammable natural materials due to their risk of igniting from popping sparks or windblown embers.

- Plan ahead for success. It's always helpful to select a shelter site that is surrounded by building materials. In a survival setting, you don't have the time or calories to waste by roaming all over the countryside to find the odd leaf or twig. Build in a place with abundant resources, like the border between forest and field, for plenty of sticks for frames, warm grasses, bedding, and other assorted construction materials. And when you build, you'll want to orient your shelter door away from prevailing winds and the likely origin of storms. This usually means facing your door to the east, avoiding the wind and storms blowing out of the west.

The Benefits of Tarp Shelters

Across the different styles of tarp shelters in this chapter, you'll find some of the same benefits among them. Here are just a few of the perks of shelters made from tarps and rope.

Speed of Construction: Tie a few corners to trees, stake a few corners to the ground, and you're done. Few shelters can be built from scratch with the speed of a tarp shelter.

Fire Safety: Your tarp shelter is a lot less flammable than a hut built from dead sticks and leaves. If you're planning on keeping a fire going all night for warmth, shelter styles like the tarp lean-to can act as a heat catcher to collect the radiant warmth from the fire. Yes, sparks can burn holes in tarps, but tarp shelters are still safer to have near a fire than any kind of debris shelters (but you don't want the fire too close to either one).

Versatility: Need a sleeping shelter in the driving rain or a sun shade with plenty of airflow underneath? The same tarp can make both. All you need are a few stakes, some rope, the odd pole or two, and your handy tarp to create many different shelter configurations.

Portability: You can't exactly throw your igloo on your back and run away, but in just a few minutes, you can untie your tarp, grab your ropes, and disappear. While they don't offer as much protection as a tent, several tarp shelter designs break down even quicker than tents.

Tarp Lean-To

The lean-to is one of the most iconic shelter styles, seen in so many books and on countless survival shows. This simple structure is easy to build, and it is very "camera-friendly," but there's more to it than that. The word "lean-to" is not a Native American name, though many people assume so. It's actually an Old English word which means a leaning shelter (it's even got "lean" in the name). Historically, the lean-to was some kind of shanty propped up against another structure, such as sticks or boards leaning against a fence or someone's medieval hovel to create storage space or provide cover for livestock. This word dates back to the fourteenth or fifteenth century British Isles, though this architectural style likely dates back to prehistoric times. Today, we often see these built with a tarp as a survival shelter, and this can be done in two main ways.

Lean-To Without a Frame

In an area with plenty of trees or bushes, you can put up a lean-to in record time using existing natural supports. By securely tying two corners of your tarp to trees and anchoring the other two corners to the ground, you're done. And in places that don't have trees, shrubs and other naturally available support structures (like some deserts and grasslands), you can use two walking sticks or trekking poles to provide your upright supports. Anchor the bottom two corners of the tarp first, then tie each of the top two corners of the tarp to the top of each pole. Tie a rope to the top of each pole and pull each rope off at an angle. Stretch each rope tight and secure the end of the rope by anchoring it to the ground (this is easier if you have one person pulling on each of the two ropes to create equal tension). In windy conditions, secure a few extra ropes to the top of each pole, pulling off in different directions for strength.

Lean-To With a Frame

This is still a simple lean-to form that can provide you with a home away from home, but it offers more strength with the addition of a wooden pole (or several). Use two pieces of rope to lash a sturdy pole horizontally between two trees. For single-pole construction, lash the top edge of the tarp at several points along this pole, then anchor the bottom edge of the tarp to the ground. For even more structural strength, place several additional poles leaning against the main pole. These can be sapling poles you have cut or dead limbs and wood you have collected from the ground. See that no sharp branches or rough bark sections will pierce your tarp. Turn the pole away from contact with the tarp or use a knife to carve these down smooth. Place them against the horizontal pole to act as "ribs," ideally on a forty-five-degree angle, then fasten down the tarp to the horizontal pole and the ground. Make sure none of the poles have rough or sharp spots that will damage or puncture your tarp, and you'll have a shelter that

performs better than a frameless lean-to. This extra effort is best suited for windy, rainy, or snowy conditions, as the poles help the tarp bear the weight of the elements.

Let the Corner Point the Way

Not sure which way to pull a rope or where to place your stakes in the ground? This is often a point of confusion for beginners. When tying ropes to tarp corners, think of the corner as an arrow, pointing in the right direction to pull the rope. The rope should come away from the tarp on a diagonal so that it applies equal tension to both tarp edges. If you anchor the rope too far off to one side or the other of this diagonal line, it will leave one of the tarp edges flapping in the wind.

A-Frame Tarp Shelter

The "A-frame" tarp shelter could go by many names, but "pup tent" is the most identifiable. This symmetrical shanty offers a lot of protection, especially when built tight to the ground, and it offers some versatility when used in creative ways. It can be suspended higher in the air, for coverage from rain that still allows airflow underneath. This higher suspension will act as a great rain fly over a hammock or any other shelter.

Start building this classic shelter by picking a good location with two trees or shrubs that can act as support. If you happen to have abundant rope, you can tie a line between the two supports and hang your tarp from the rope almost like a clothesline. If rope is scarce, use a short piece of rope to tie from each edge of the tarp to the supports and

simply pull the tarp tight between the supports. Once the tarp is hanging with two equal "wings," pull out the four corners, one at a time, and stake them to the ground. One of the best aspects of this style is the amount of coverage you get from such a quickly built shelter. Once you familiarize yourself with the style (and pick a good shelter site), you can get your tarp hung in ten minutes or less. You can even use a poncho as an A-frame tarp shelter.

Success With Stakes

It would be great if you could use strong slender stakes right through the grommet holes (those metal or plastic reinforcing rings) to anchor the bottom edge of a tarp to

(continued next page)

the ground, but it doesn't usually work out like this. If the stake is slender enough to go through the grommet hole, it's usually too short and spindly to be sturdy. And if you have to carve your own stakes from sticks, they probably won't fit through the grommet holes either. The solution to securing the bottom edge of the tarp to the ground with stakes is to use short sections of cord to connect the stake and the hole in the tarp. This way, you can use larger and stronger stakes, since they no longer need to fit through the available grommet ring.

Diamond Fly Tarp Shelter

One of my favorites; this aerodynamic shape delivers protection from wind and windblown rain, and it's relatively quick to set up and adjust. Build this sleek shelter by tying one tarp corner to a tree or similar support, then anchoring the opposing corner to the ground. This opposite corner on the ground should be pulled tight and pointed into the wind. You don't want the wind to blow into the large "doorway" of this shelter (or any other). Once the two opposing corners are secured, tie out the other two corners to stakes or other anchors. For more complete protection, you can even add another tarp as a door or hang up a blanket for complete coverage. In preparation for bad weather, this shelter (and any of the others) can be further secured with additional tie-downs as needed.

Tie Without a Corner Grommet

It happens all the time. The little brass or plastic grommet ring in the corner of a tarp will tear out, leaving you without a place to attach a rope. Don't worry, there's an easy solution, and it only involves a strange knot: the sheet bend. This old sailing knot can connect the rope to the tarp, without the use of any holes in the tarp. To tie it, bunch up the corner of the tarp and "bend" it to form a "J" shape. Run the rope through the curve of the "J," coming from behind. Wrap the rope around the entire "J" shape. Tuck the rope under itself (don't go back down through the "J," this won't hold). Finish the knot by pulling on the "tail" of the rope—the knot

(continued next page)

will compress the tarp and bite into it. Oddly enough, this knot is often stronger than the grommet it replaces.

Tarp Hammock

If you've got a strong tarp that can hold some weight, and similarly strong rope, you can use the sheet bend knot that we already shared to create an improvised hammock between two trees. This elevated shelter can put some space between you and the ground in areas that are wet, or places that are crawling with pests and hazardous animals. I'd recommend using an eight-by-ten-foot tarp and sturdy rope, at least ¼ inch in diameter (or a thicker rope for larger hammock occupants). Get your tarp ready by laying it out flat on the ground. Take the edge of one of the long sides and begin to roll it up like a scroll. Roll the side evenly and stop once you've rolled it halfway across the entire tarp. Next, roll up the opposing long side, rolling it toward the center of the tarp. Once the rolling is complete, your tarp should look like two

rolls of plastic or canvas that are side by side and ten feet long. Next, take one of your rolled ends and bend it to make the "J" shape needed for a sheet bend knot. Run the end of a rope piece through the "J" and around the outside, finishing by tucking the rope under itself. For added security, tie an overhand knot in the rope to act as a "stopper knot," which will keep the rope from slipping through the "J" turn. Using a second piece of rope, tie another sheet bend on the other side of the tarp. Now, choose the trees you'll use to suspend the hammock. They should be "leg thick" or larger for strength, and located about ten feet apart. Use strong knots to tie each rope to each tree, as high as you can reach on the trunk. Tying this high on the trees compensates for the extra rope length you'll get as the sheet bends to settle. Tying lower to the trees would likely mean that your finished hammock will be dragging the ground once everything stretches. Once the ropes are tied securely to the trees, partially unroll the two rolled tarp edges and gradually apply body weight to set the knots. You can finish the hammock by tying up another tarp as a rain fly over the hammock, or just crawl into it and enjoy it as it hangs.

Keep the Hammock to Yourself

Sharing has it's time and place, but the last thing you'll want to share is your hammock with an assortment of the local wildlife. Try these techniques for keeping the tarp hammock free of unwanted visitors.

Use a Covering: Whether you are in the hammock or out working, you'll want to keep the hammock covered to protect it from creatures that like to drop out of trees. This could be done by flinging another tarp over the hammock so that it's not sitting there like a bowl to catch spiders and other pests. Better yet, you could string up a second tarp in an A-frame or wing shelter style between the two trees holding the hammock. This will act as a critter barrier and a rain fly overhead.

Cut Them Off: Limiting the access to your hammock is also helpful. The two main ropes holding up your hammock are indispensable, but try limiting the other points of attachment. For example, instead of tying six ropes to your rain

(continued next page)

fly, see if four will do the job. This will reduce the access points that snakes, insects, spiders, and other unwelcomed creatures could use to crawl into the hammock.

Repel Them: I'm not going to walk through a bunch of kerosene, and most animals won't either. By tying a rag onto each hammock line that has been dribbled with kerosene or diesel fuel (or some other slow-drying noxious fuel), no self-respecting bugs, spiders, rats, or other creepy crawlies will slink down your ropes to get into your hammock. Just make sure you keep any open flames away from the fuel-soaked cloth.

Desert Tarp

When it comes to blocking the burning rays of the sun and their accompanying heat, two tarps are better than one. The idea of having a double-layered roof dates back hundreds of years in the hotter regions of the earth, particularly in some parts of Africa and the Middle East. And in more recent years, a two-tarp desert shelter has found widespread notoriety in various military survival training programs. This "double-roofed" shelter can provide a much cooler place to hide from the midday sun than just a single tarp. Its effectiveness is thanks to the insulating pocket of dead air space between the two tarps. The air temperature underneath this contraption may be lower than the surrounding air temperature by 10 to 20 degrees Fahrenheit. To build one for yourself, you'll need two tarps (ideally the same size) and several dozen feet of rope. This works best when you take advantage of the natural coolness of the ground, and you build over a low spot or you dig a shallow pit in the ground (before the day gets hot). Start the build by laying one tarp over the low spot and securing it using stakes, poles,

or standing stones as well as a rope from each corner to some kind of anchor. Using whatever spacers you can muster (being very careful if using rocks, which could fall out of place easily if the tarps flap in the wind), secure the second tarp above the first tarp, leaving one foot of air space between the two tarps. This doubled roof can also be built using a large rectangular tarp, folded in half to make the two layers.

Use a Sandbag

For loose sandy terrain that won't hold slender stakes in the ground, try some sandbags for anchors. Ordinary plastic grocery bags are commonly found as trash across the planet, but by filling one with sand and tying a rope to both handles, you'll have an anchor option that is fast and much more reliable than thin tent stakes. For best results, "double bag" each sandbag and bury them in holes so that the wind cannot shift them.

Tarp Teepee

Teepee shelters are heavily associated with the nomadic Native American cultures of the American Great Plains, though these cone-shaped homes can be found around the globe. The teepee (also written as tipi and tepee), is made from a ring of poles that act as a conical frame, and some type of covering that blocks the weather. In former times, this covering was laboriously made of buffalo hide, and today they are often made of canvas. A teepee can be any size, and most work very effectively as natural chimneys when a fire is lit in the center and a smoke vent is incorporated in the design. To make your own teepee from one or more tarps, you'll need sturdy yet slender poles and some kind of tarp material. This could be parachute material, plastic or canvas tarps, ship's sails, or anything else that fits the purpose. To make it, tie the ends of three poles together and raise them up like a tripod. Rest your additional poles between the "forks" of the initial tripod and space them evenly. Wrap your tarp (or several tarps) around the conical frame and tie them down securely. When possible, make the tarp edges come together to create a door flap, which can be closed in cold or wet weather.

Tarp Burrito

When you're short on time (or lacking the support structures to pitch a tent-like tarp shelter), the tarp burrito is your fastest option to get out of the rain. Don't expect this shelter option to be comfortable; it's not. And don't expect a lot of room; you won't have much. The part that matters is the fact that you can set it up in a minute or less.

Just lay your tarp on the ground in a safe shelter location. Fold one side of the tarp over onto itself, folding it about one-third of the way across the tarp. Then fold the doubled section over again in the same direction. This creates a tube-like tarp with the free edge underneath. Now tuck one of the two open ends of the tarp underneath (just as you'd fold the end under to make a burrito), and this will only leave one opening for the tube. Slide your sleeping bag down into the tarp

tube and crawl inside, feet first. By making these folds, the tarp is wrapped around you and pinned beneath your body weight (except for the door opening). You can allow this opening in the burrito to flop down in stormy weather, or you can hold the opening up with a bit of rope and some vertical support. Keep in mind that nothing is this fast and simple without problems. The burrito tarp shelter has very little ventilation, especially with the opening flopped down. This means that there will usually be a buildup of moisture inside the burrito from water vapor coming off your body during the night. It's also a very claustrophobic shelter, with little room for storage. This is just a quick way to get out of the weather, and a temporary respite at best.

Tarp Wing

For blocking sun or gentle rain, this unorthodox tarp shelter is easy to set up and is roomy underneath. I routinely use a large twenty-by-forty-foot tarp in this style to create a rain shelter high over my campfire during

wilderness classes, but this configuration is also useful for coverage over smaller areas (like a hammock). Create this easy shelter by tying the opposing corners of a tarp to two trees or some other supports. Tie the next two opposing corners to ropes and anchor them to the ground. The end result should be two corners supported high and two corners in going down. This shape is prone to being torn in higher winds, but it works well to keep off both sun and rain in calmer weather.

Bury a "Deadman"

There are several conditions when driving stakes into the ground just isn't an option. When the ground is full of rocks, you can bend metal stakes and shatter wooden ones by trying to pound them in, and in loose shifting sand or dry snow, stakes will pull right back out when any tension is applied to the rope. Here's the best option—create a "deadman" anchor. By using a short section of log or an elongated rock, you can fasten your rope to the center of the object and keep it perpendicular to the rope. If heavy enough, this object can lie there on its own as an anchor. You could also pile rocks or other log sections on top for additional support, or in true "deadman" style, you could bury the object in the soil, sand, or snow. Just move the object to pull the rope tight before you anchor it down for good.

Wedge Tarp

Similar to the diamond fly shelter, the wedge tarp shelter in one of the most low-drag designs you can build, and it's ideally suited to cut through strong wind and shed heavy rain. You'll have your best results with this tarp shelter when the prevailing winds blow from a constant direction, though the "flaps" can be lowered if the wind does shift. To build the wedge tarp shelter, stake down two corners of the tarp into the wind (not opposing corners; stake down adjacent corners). Then tie up a line to the center of the opposite side of the tarp. Tie the remaining two corners down toward the ground. You can use more cord and set your anchors farther away to have open wings and better ventilation. You could also tie the last corners down to stakes in the ground that are close to the shelter to draw the "flaps" downward for more coverage and weatherproofing. With a minimum of five tie-down points and low profile, the wedge is one of the most likely shelters to survive a storm without damage.

Make a "Wart"

When there's no secure ring in the corner of a tarp, you've seen how the sheet bend knot can come in handy. But what happens when you need to fasten a rope to a tarp and you are not on a corner? Pick up a hard nut or small round pebble from the ground and place it under the tarp where you need to create an attachment. Wrap the tarp tightly around the nut or stone to create a bump in the material. This is commonly called a "wart." Tie your rope tightly around the base of this lump in the tarp and pull the rope to test it. It shouldn't move. You can make a "wart" attachment anywhere on a tarp. You can even make a series of warts in the corners of a tarp if you are having trouble using the sheet bend.

5

Shelters from Vegetation

Before the time of tarps and tents, and in the absence of a nice cave, our ancestors learned to build their homes from the vegetation around them. Using all types of natural building materials, homes sprung up that suited the environment and the raw resources at hand. This practice of making huts from plant materials may have begun out of simple necessity, when other building materials (like hides) were scarce. It may have also been a purposeful shift in construction materials. In a predator-rich world, living in a hut covered with rotting animal hides would create a near-constant draw to scavenging animals and predators. Sure, these plant-based buildings were more of a fire hazard than hide-covered homes, but the shift may have very well played a role in our prosperity as a species. Today, a working knowledge of the diverse shelter styles of our forebears can still prove useful in a survival setting. For those who are lost in a woodland environment, an ax, saw, or your bare hands can give you access to a variety of shelter building materials. The forest can provide branches, poles, and logs to erect strong shelter frames. The dead tree leaves and evergreen boughs can become a roofing material or soft bedding. Bark slabs can even be used as shingles to repel water and block the wind. Similarly, jungles and grasslands can provide a wealth of building supplies for roofs, walls, beds, platforms, and other shelter components. All it takes is some creativity and adaptability to turn the materials you have into the structures you need. The best part about it is that these skills are "evergreen." That is to say, the art of making shelters from vegetation has always worked for us, and it will always work.

Lean-To

In Chapter Four, "Tarp Shelters," you learned about the lean-to and how to make that shelter style using a tarp, but what happens when you need a quick shelter and you don't have a tarp to build it? The lean-to can also be built from natural materials, without a single modern resource. Just a few strong poles, some long sticks, and a mound of vegetation are the necessary components of this classic backwoods shelter. Here's how to build one of your own.

Build the Frame

Start out by choosing a safe shelter spot with things that will provide strong structural support. I don't recommend building a vegetation lean-to with a pair of tripods for support. This will work when using a tarp for the weatherproofing, but the massive weight of the vegetation and sticks (plus the weight of rain or snow), will create something closer to a deadfall trap than a shelter if you set it up as a freestanding shelter. In a woodland environment, I prefer to use two trees as my supports, though you can also use stumps, boulders, and other immobile objects. Once you've chosen your supports, select a long, heavy

pole that will span the distance and act as a horizontal beam. The thinnest part of the pole should be at least three inches in diameter, and it should not be rotten wood or a brittle species. This can be tied to the two trees with reliable rope, or you can use a pair of forked posts to hold the beam in place against the tree trunks. Finish the frame by covering the leaning side with sticks and poles, with about two inches of space between them or even tighter (to keep debris from falling through). These are the "ribs" of the structure, and they can be clean straight saplings cut from the nearby area or they can be dead branches collected from the ground and broken into the right lengths. For best results, set the ribs up somewhere near a forty-five-degree angle. This provides a good balance between rain defense and providing a covered space. If the angle is steeper, there won't be much room underneath the shelter. If the angle is not steep enough, you'll have more roof weight on the support beam (maybe enough to break it), and you'll have more rain dripping through.

Add the Roofing

Once your ribs are in place against the horizontal beam, you can begin adding the materials to create a makeshift roof. Start at the bottom of the wall, mounding up any available vegetation and working upward. You could use dead leaves, loose pine needles, evergreen boughs, grasses, palm fronds, ferns, or any other vegetation you can cut down or rake up. In the right climate, you may even be able to cut thick sheets of moss from the ground and stack them like a wall. These various materials can be wet or dry, alive or dead, as long as they divert the rain and block the wind. You can also add something extra to block the weather. Fresh-cut or dead bark slabs can be placed on top of the roof to act like modern shingles. These can be laid down randomly, or better yet, overlapped like Spanish tiles. These add extra water resistance, and they prevent the wind from blowing the leaves off the shelter roof.

Using a Fire With the Lean-To

The biggest flaw of the lean-to is that it can't hold in any heat. It's a lot like having a house with only one wall and half of a roof. This means that you'll get cold under there without a mountain of insulation piled underneath its overhang—or you'll need a fire nearby for warmth. We typically build most shelters with the opening facing out of the prevailing winds for better weather protection, but this can cause smoke to swirl under the shelter when the wind blows over it. A better solution when the wind direction is constant is to build the lean-to's long axis parallel to the wind. This allows the wind to blow the smoke away rather than pushing it into the shelter. Build an elongated fire that runs parallel to the lean-to and keep the fire about ten feet away from the shelter for fire safety.

Build Against a Wall

The lean-to originated as a simple shelter propped up against a wall, and this can still be a useful trick. Large boulders and rock walls can act as your support system for a lean-to, and you can build a closed-in shelter by simply propping the rib sticks up against the wall. Structurally, you're making the same pieces, but a lean-to built against two trees will have an open side exposed to the weather. By building the lean-to propped against a wall, you'll now have an enclosed shelter with more weather protection.

Leaf Hut Shelter

When you need more protection and warmth than a lean-to can provide, try the two-sided leaf hut. This wedge-shaped lodge offers more weather resistance and a much warmer place to sleep than many other brush shelters. Think of it as a "people nest," and you're on the right track. This shelter uses a thick mound of vegetation to create dead air space around your body, thereby keeping you protected from the wind, rain, snow, and cold temperatures. These can also be built with your bare hands and the materials that nature provides, so don't worry if you forgot your chain saw. When built thick enough, you won't even need a sleeping bag or blanket inside it for warmth. This one shelter does it all.

Frame It up

Start your build by finding a long pole to act as the "backbone" of the shelter. It should be about ten to fourteen feet long. The lighter end can be propped in the fork of a tree (if you find a fork at a convenient height). You could also prop it up on a boulder or a stump for support. My preferred method, however, is to use a pair of forked prop sticks to hold the pole. Each forked stick should be about three feet long and very sturdy. When propped up, it should look like a tripod with one extra-long leg. However you set up this pole, test it for strength by putting some bodyweight on it. There should be no chance of this frame breaking or falling apart. Next, you'll need to cover both sides of the pole with materials that will act as ribs. These could be stiff bark slabs, sticks, and dead branches, or even fresh-cut tree boughs. These are broken or cut to length, then placed along each side of the hut to frame up the walls. It's helpful to crawl inside during construction, to ensure that you'll fit into the finished shelter but it's not too roomy. Place the ribs close together so that the debris can't fall between them and break

them off so that none of the sticks will poke a hole through the finished roof of debris. If ribs are left too long, they will create gaps in the roof material—allowing rain to drip in and heat to escape.

Cover It Over

With the framework complete, it's time to cover the structure. Like the lean-to, you can use almost any plant material that can trap air, shed rain, and block wind. This could be dead or green grasses, dead or green leaves, ferns, moss, or pine needles. In a location with sparse vegetation, you could even cut brush and weeds or break down tree boughs. Oddly enough, this material can be dry or wet, live or dead. Just remember that green materials will probably wilt and compact as they die, leaving less volume and less dead air space. By collecting dead material from the landscape, the insulation value won't change, and your presence will be less destructive. Using dead materials is ideal for practice settings, but if you're in a real emergency, don't hesitate to use any materials you need to use. And whichever materials you have, you'll have at least two feet of vegetation covering all sides of the shelter for minimal protection, though a three-foot thick layer is more effective. As it stands, your two- to three-foot roof of leaves is enough to keep you dry, and if you have a sleeping bag and a pad to go under it, you're done. If you get caught without bedding, this shelter is a lot like an empty tent. It's capable of blocking the wind, rain, and snow, but you'll still freeze to death inside without insulation around your body. That's why we add more vegetation in the form of bedding.

Add the Bedding

This is the part that will make all the difference for warmth. You'll need to fill the interior of the shelter with leaves or other debris, and because this compresses when you lay on it, you'll need to stuff it multiple times. Pack the complete interior cavity with debris, filled all the way up to the roof beam and remembering all the corners (these corners can become "cold spots" if ignored). To compress it, crawl in feet first and lay on it. Crawl out and stuff the remaining space with more debris. Lay on this as well, and then fill the remaining space a third time. Leave this third stuffing in place, creating two layers of compressed vegetation underneath you (as a mattress) and one fluffy layer covering you. It's also helpful to leave a pile of debris just outside the door, which can be used to plug the door, to fill in gaps you find in the middle of the night, or as a pillow.

Make the Finishing Touches

You may not realize it during the build, but there's one small touch that will make a big difference in your shelter. This is a door that can close the triangular shelter opening. This item should never be anything heavy, like a slab of flat rock, which could fall on your head as you enter, exit, or sleep. A large lightweight bark slab would be much safer, yet still block the wind and some of the heat loss. Better yet, you can build a door. Cut some flexible green sticks and make two woven mats that are slightly larger than your opening, yet match the shape. Pile up some leaves or grass on one mat and place the second mat on top for a debris "sandwich." Use cord or a flexible vine to lash the two mats together and you'll have a lightweight insulated door to protect you in the coldest weather.

Beat the Wind

In the event of high winds, debris such as leaves and grass can be stripped right off the hut without something to hold them down. This can be a generous layer of bark slabs, as discussed in the lean-to section. You can also cover the exterior of the hut with a layer of lightweight brush, sticks, twigs, or branches. There's no need to weave them together. Just lay them around the dome of vegetation and they will form a cage that will prevent the wind from stripping your debris away.

Shingle Your Roof

Natural shelters from vegetation don't have to be all one material, like 100 percent grass or leaves. It's better to mix building materials and utilize the best features of each. Take dead bark slabs, for example. Their corky content does trap dead air space, and they can be used as a rudimentary mattress to get you off the ground, but my favorite use for them is shingles. By stacking bark pieces on the roof, overlapping just like modern roof shingles, any natural shelter will resist the wind and rain better. You can even interlock them, like Spanish tiles, with some running concave side up and others covering the gaps, concave side down. Just make sure your structure can support the weight, if you choose to use a lot of them (they'll get even heavier when wet). But even one solid dead bark piece would be useful on a roof, creating at least one spot where the moisture will run off.

Wickiup

This ubiquitous shelter style isn't specific to any one culture, time period, or region, since it can be seen around the world. The name, however, and its most common occurrence are documented in the American Southwest. The wickiup is a form of natural material shelter constructed from a cone of sturdy poles and covered in brush or any other local vegetation (earning it the nickname "brush teepee"). Of course, if you had the buffalo hides—like the ancient teepee builders used—you could fashion something with better wind and rain resistance (and it would even be portable). For our purposes, it makes more sense to focus on the materials that are most common

and brush is easier to find than hides. Start your build by choosing a practical location and assembling a very strong tripod of poles. These could be tied together, or you could use forked sticks that interlock. Add additional poles around the structure, encircling at least two-thirds of the "teepee" ring. Placing poles around three-fourths of the perimeter would be even more sturdy, but never go around less than two-thirds of the way. This will create a very lopsided structure that may collapse. Place the poles close enough together that your chosen brush or vegetation can't fall through. Finish the exterior with a layer of brush, leaves, or any other vegetation you can collect. When the wickiup is large enough, and the vegetation is either wet or green material (not too flammable), you may even be able to get away with a tiny fire inside the shelter (built from wood that produces few sparks). You can change the design a little for different climates. For example, building a broader, squattier structure that is lightly covered with brush will yield a shady, ventilated shelter for hot and dry climates. Using a steeper roof pitch and building with thick brush or grass thatching will make the shelter perform better in the rain.

Wigwam

In former times, many of our ancestors used large sheets of bark to cover their wilderness homes. Starting in the warmth of spring, bark naturally separates from the wood underneath it. This odd condition of loose bark persists until midsummer, then the bark attaches back tight against the wood. During this time, the bark can be cut into sections and peeled off to be used as a covering for wigwams and longhouses. These bark sheets can be taken off in large or small sizes, then flattened out and dried for use as a wall and roofing material.

Collect the Materials

This build begins with the cutting of flexible saplings to create a shelter frame, and the peeling of bark to cover that frame. For a small wigwam, cut thirty hardwood saplings that are at least twelve to fifteen feet tall. You'll also need to fell two medium-sized trees with flexible bark. In my home area, we use tulip poplar trees for this, though other species will work. Cut the bark into large rectangular slabs and score some diagonal scratch marks on the inner side of the bark. This allows it to be flattened out with less chance of cracking. Slack the bark and place heavy rocks on top of the stack to flatten them out. Allow them to dry for several days or even a few weeks to encourage their flattening. You'll also need hundreds of yards of cordage for this build, though this can be strips of flexible inner bark instead of twisted rope.

Build the Dome

Using small sticks, mark out a circle on the ground, sticking in twelve sticks in a circle, roughly ten to twelve feet in diameter. Carve a stake from a hardwood stick and use a large rock as a hammer to drive the stake into the ground when your twelve sticks mark the spot. Each time you drive in the stake, go about one foot deep, wiggle the stake around, and pull it out. This creates a hole for the end of each sapling to go into. Ideally, the stake should be the same size as the thicker part of your saplings, each sapling should be the same thickness, and the hole should angle outward from the shelter circle. Leaning the holes outward is important, since the soil will compact a little after the saplings are tied to each other. By leaning the holes outward, the finished product will be straight vertical walls. If the holes were straight vertical to begin with, the finished walls would lean inward, and this is not preferred. Once the holes in the ground have been made, insert a sapling in each hole and do your best to force it down to the bottom of each hole. With

all twelve saplings sunk into the ground, choose two opposing ones and bend them down to meet. For example, bring the "three o'clock" sapling and the "nine o'clock" sapling together. Adjust the shape and height of your first arch, then lash the two saplings together. Repeat this until all the saplings are tied to their opposite sapling. Decide where you want your door (typically facing east) and mark the spot. Now, take your remaining saplings and begin to lash them horizontally around your dome, leaving the doorway open. With every overlapping pair of saplings tied, the dome will look like a cage. It will be flexible, but it is still very strong.

Cover It with Bark

Now comes the hardest part: trying to put together the bark jigsaw puzzle. By twisting a knife tip or small drill, carefully drill holes in the corners of the bark slabs and start stitching them onto the shelter frame. Start at the bottom and work your way upward, overlapping like shingles. Don't hesitate to drill more holes around the edges of the bark to fasten sections that are loose, bulging, or otherwise ill-fitting. You may have to get on someone's shoulders to work on the upper parts, or work from inside the structure to reach the roof. Leave an opening in the center for a smoke hole (if you intend to have a fire inside), and you are almost done with your build.

Finish the Job

A door would be a great addition and could be made from bark, as well. A smoke hole cover would be another useful bark item, to cover the roof opening during very bad weather or absences from the shelter. But there's one thing that's even more important than those shelter facets: It's the outer cage of saplings. Without this extra layer of sapling support, the bark sheets will not lay flat, regardless of the number of holes you drill and ties you tighten. Run saplings around the bottom edge of the shelter exterior (these can be tied or held in place with stakes in the ground). To compress the bark tight against the inner shelter frame, run more vertical and horizontal saplings, as well. Ideally, you can drill holes to stitch the inner frame and outer frame together so that they sandwich the bark in between. Just be aware that the bark will curl up without this cage, and it's a vital part of the build.

Add Some Benches

I'm not sure why, but adding benches inside a wigwam or longhouse is the most satisfying part of the build for me. Working off of the inner frame of the wigwam, I'll drive a number of stout forked stakes into the ground so that their forks are about fifteen to eighteen inches off the ground. I'll lay poles in these forks and create a matching horizontal pole lashed onto the shelter wall. Between these poles, I'll make rows of short sticks that span the gap and lash them all in place. This bench system can wrap around the entire shelter interior or be made in sections. Benches offer storage underneath, seating and sleeping areas on top. Add some furs or mats for comfort and light the fire to feel like home.

Build with Dead Bark

When larger trees were more plentiful in the world, peeling the bark from a few of them to build a home didn't have much impact on the environment. Today, we can still use bark for low impact survival shelters by scaling down the size of the lodge and by only using dead bark. By prying the bark from fallen trees in stiff slabs, we won't have such a flexible building material but can use the rigid bark pieces over a teepee-style frame, thus creating a bark-covered shelter similar to a wickiup.

Add a Vegetation Bed

We can't say that this is a shelter all by itself, but it's a great addition to a lean-to, wickiup, and some roomier shelter types. It's also something you can make from many different plant materials. I frequently use dead leaves to make primitive shelter beds, although grasses, pine needles,

(continued next page)

ferns, evergreen boughs, and other plant material will work, too. Some of these materials are a little prickly, such as cedar and some pine boughs, while fir and hemlock pine boughs make a very soft bed. Try it out for yourself. Create the bed frame by rolling up two logs that are a little longer than you are tall. Place these under your shelter side by side, roughly three feet apart. If they seem to shift, use angular rocks to "chock" them to prevent rolling, or drive small stakes into the ground to "peg" the logs into position. Once the two logs are set, fill the void between them with your preferred vegetation. Each time you fill the space, lay down on the material to compact it. Repeat this several times until the "mattress" is at least six inches thick when you are lying on it.

Cover with Mats

Bark isn't your only option for covering a wigwam. Large mats can be woven from reeds, cattail plants, and other vegetation to offer weather protection on these shelters. It will take a large volume of cordage to put these mats together, and a significant amount of time. It's much more environmentally friendly to cut vegetation that will grow back in a few months than to kill and skin trees that take one hundred years to grow back. Mats can also be used in areas that lack suitable bark for wigwams. These mats can be woven in many different ways, though you'll have your fastest production by creating a simple loom. Drive a row of sturdy stakes into the ground and tie two long strings to each one. Jam a bundle of long leafed vegetation between the pairs of strings and then tie the pairs of strings around the bundle to lock it in place. Keep adding bundles and tying them into the strings. Mats will usually last about a year when exposed to the sun and weather, so your mat-covered wigwam would need to be replaced each year—usually in the summer. Mats can also be used as an "under layer" with bark sheets attached overtop for a durable combination of weatherproofing and insulation.

6
Snow Shelters

Finding shelter in a landscape full of snow and ice may seem like an unwinnable war, but just because things look bleak doesn't mean all is lost. Millennia ago, people living in the far North discovered the secrets of using snow as a shelter material. As the generations passed down this information, refinements and new tools allowed us to look at snow as a savior instead of just a killer. From the sophisticated and elegant igloo, still built today by our cousins near the Arctic Circle, to the simple survival shelters scratched out of snowbanks, snow is more than just a frozen hazard. It's a building block and insulator, perfect for buffering the intense cold and wind chill of frigid conditions. Perhaps our ancestors learned what to do by watching animals dig snow caves to hibernate through the winter, or perhaps they just discovered it for themselves. Either way, snow may be cold to the touch, but it's a good insulator. Fresh snow is the best, consisting of a high percentage of air trapped among the flakes. It's typically 90 to 95 percent air and 5 to 10 percent water. Once the air becomes trapped, it can't move much or transfer heat as well as moving air. And as you dig down into the snow, you'll find that the snowpack is warmer. In deep snow, the top foot or two will reflect the air temperatures. Closer to the ground, the deeper snowpack will be warmer due to the warmth of the earth. So after all is said and done, snow isn't the enemy it appears to be—the one that freezes your skin and hides the sticks and leaves you wanted to build a shelter with. Snow is a building material, an insulator, a drinking water source, and so much more.

Find a Tree Well Shelter

Occasionally, your good luck and bad luck will mix. You might experience some bad luck, such as getting caught overnight in a forest with deep snow but finding a ready-made shelter that nature provided. In evergreen forests that have had deep snowfall, the trees themselves can form naturally occurring shelters. Frequently called tree wells, these openings occur when the snow clings to the boughs of a large evergreen tree, instead of piling up underneath the tree. This natural pit in the snow can act as a shelter all by itself or be modified for additional protection. As you travel through forested environments in the colder months, you may notice that certain tree species are naturally better than others for creating tree wells. You may also notice that certain areas are more likely to create this formation in the winter. For best results as a survival shelter, dig through any snow until you hit the bare frozen ground. You can use this excavated snow to plug any gaps or build a wall around the edge of the snow pit. You won't want to disturb the snow on the boughs above the tree well, but you can break off or cut the boughs from neighboring trees to place as an insulating layer on the floor of this pit. This layer is vital to prevent conductive heat loss into the ground as you sit or lie down in the tree well. Make these boughs as thick as possible, and shake off the snow before bringing them down into the pit. These boughs can also be used as wall material or even a door, when stuck into the snow or piled up.

Avoid Mixing Fire and Ice

It may seem like a glorious idea to put a fire down in a tree well or inside an igloo, and if the smoke doesn't choke you, it may feel great for just a little while. But at some point, the warmth of a fire will begin to melt your precious insulating snow, and at some point, it's coming down on your fire (and maybe your head). In a tree well, the fire will melt the snow-covered boughs overhead, and drop a load of slush on your fire. In an all-snow shelter, you'll melt a hole in your ceiling or collapse the whole thing. For greater warmth in shelters made from snow, pack them full of insulating materials, like leaves and green boughs, to make the most of your body heat and leave the fire outside. And if that's not enough, burn a fire outside to warm up stones. These can provide warmth inside your snow shelter by placing them directly underneath your coats and clothing, which will warm *you* rather than heating the air inside a snow shelter.

Carve Your Own Cave

Yes, the wind and snow can give you hypothermia and kill you, but they can also create the perfect conditions to hollow out a sheltered spot in the frozen landscape. When windblown snow creates deep drifts—which freeze into a stable mass—these are the ideal parameters to dig your own snow cave. Planning ahead for the possibility of this shelter is smart, and bringing a shovel is even smarter, though you can

certainly excavate this refuge with improvised digging tools. A solid body snowshoe, a large cook pot, a plank of wood, or even your gloved hands can be used to dig out the snow cave. To start, create a small round tunnel, low in the drift, and then spread the excavation up and to the sides. If possible, pick a place on the drift where you can throw your loose snow downhill rather than uphill; this will save a surprising amount of energy as you work. Dig out a section that is higher to create a raised sleeping platform. You'll also want to add one or more ventilation holes as you work—for airflow and to check the snow thickness. Leave your entrance tunnel low with a vacant area that will act as a "cold well." This gives colder air a place to sink and settle as it drifts away from the raised sleeping platform. As you finalize the cave's shape and size, keep the walls vertical and let the ceiling be round. This "domed" ceiling is much more secure than a flat ceiling. For convenience, you can dig shelves or niches in the walls and stab sticks into the walls to hang things. Pile up a deep mattress of evergreen boughs or other insulating material on your sleeping platform as a mattress. Before you call it a night, mark the roof of the cave or block the area off to keep anyone from walking up there and causing a cave-in. You'll also want to keep your shovel or digging tool inside the cave, just in case you need to dig your way out. Block the doorway with a backpack or a block of snow that can act as a door.

Build a Quinzee

Sometimes called the "poor man's igloo," the quinzee is not a commonly built shelter, but it does suit certain conditions. Also spelled "quinzhee," the word comes to us from the Athabaskan languages of Canada, through this type of shelter has also been known as a *lumitalo* in Finland. Whatever you call it, this shelter is not suited for loose snows or snow that must be cut into blocks. It's best made when you have a heavy snowfall of wet packable snow, usually at temperatures closer to

the freezing mark (rather than deep sub-freezing cold). Since this shelter takes a lot more physical labor than scratching out a snow cave or crawling into a ready-made tree well, the quinzee is best built as a small group shelter, taking advantage of the extra labor force and plenty of body heat for nighttime warmth. The easiest way to begin your build is to pile up your gear (like backpacks and bags) and cover them with a tarp or poncho. The bigger the pile, the better this trick will work. If a tarp was available but baggage was lacking, you could also throw a tarp over a mound of loose snow. Next, scoop up all of the surrounding snow and create a large snow mound over your tarp. Pack the snow down on top of the pile tightly, and as you work, insert a good number of sticks around the mound. Your sticks should all be the same length, roughly twelve to eighteen inches long. These will act like "rebar," stabilizing the structure, and they also act as convenient depth gauges to create uniform thickness in the dome. If you have the time to spare, let your snow mound freeze and harden for a few hours before moving to the next step—excavation. Dig out a small doorway and continue burrowing into the mound until you hit your tarp. Lift the tarp and remove the gear to quickly create a cavity. Continue working by excavating this as if it were a snow cave. Stop digging away the snow when you begin to find the bottoms of the sticks. Finish the job by using a backpack as a door and add one or two small vent holes for fresh air.

Cut a Snow Trench

For those who happen to be carrying a saw into the frozen wastelands but lack the engineering skills to build an igloo, the snow trench might just be your next best option. When the snow base is packed well enough to saw into pieces, the snow can be cut out as slabs and used as building materials. By cutting the blocks out of the snow pack, you're actually getting two things: Sawing the blocks and removing them forms the

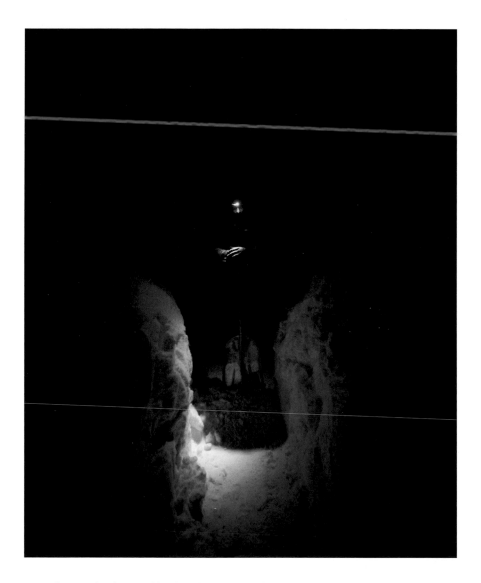

trench in which you'll take shelter. It also gives you the blocks to create a roof over the trench. For best results, orient the trench perpendicular to the prevailing wind so it's not whistling through your shelter. You'll also want to pre-cut the angles on the block edges that will rest against each other. It's also helpful to stagger the blocks for structural strength and include a shelf along the trench edge for the block bases to set into.

To finish the shelter, block off one end with a triangular snow block and fill any gaps with snow. Cut out one final block that will act as a door, and heavily line the bottom of the trench with insulation of some kind. Evergreen boughs are a great choice, as these can be found above the snow. Just make it very thick to keep your body heat from conducting down into the snow below you. This simple shelter is often one of your better choices in flat snowy areas, and it is best suited as a one-man or two-man shelter from the cold.

Dig a Snow Pit

When the snow cannot be cut into slabs or packed together, a shovel, some sticks, and something to cover the sticks are all you need to make a modified version of the snow trench shelter, ideal for one person in need of a quick shelter. This shelter won't be roomy, but it could save your life in a pinch. To build this version, dig a ramp down into the snow and excavate a trench that is a bit wider and longer than you would be when lying down. Pile the loose snow on one side, as you'll need it for coverage later. Then fill the trench with as many evergreen boughs as you need to create a mattress. Keep in mind that the boughs will compress a lot when lying on them, so more greenery is better than less. Once your "mattress" is done, lay a series of sticks or poles across the trench, and then cover them with evergreen boughs or a tarp. Mound the roof over with the loose snow as an insulating layer and devise a door of some kind to hold in your heat. This door could be a backpack that plugs the opening, or you could create something from woven evergreen boughs to seal the entrance.

Make an Igloo

Laying the blocks for a legitimate igloo will take some skill and patience, but if you can successfully pull it off, the sturdy spiraling

dome is the ultimate in survival engineering. If built in the correct way with the right snow, just a candle or a little body heat can render the interior temperature hospitable, even if the environment outside of the igloo is uninhabitable. Begin by finding well-packed snow that can be cut into blocks. Start with forming a triangular block, then move on to making trapezoidal blocks, all with tapered edges. Overlap the joints for strength, just as brick or cinderblock walls are made (you never see all the joints in vertical straight lines). Cut the blocks smaller as you near completion, and cut the final block as the "key" piece in the center of the ceiling. Like a snow cave, you'll want to include an upward reaching entryway, a "cold well," a door, ventilation holes, and a sleeping platform—at a minimum. We don't have room to go into all the subtleties or the long history of igloos here. This is a very glib explanation of a very complex art form, and igloo building is a true legacy skill. Suffice it to say that someone with a rudimentary understanding of geometry, some patience, and a little construction experience can make a passable igloo, given enough time and forgiving snow.

Make a Dry Bed in Snowy Terrain

Even though snow is loaded with dead air space that creates a certain level of insulation, a pile of snow is hardly suitable for a bed. So what can you use in a snow-covered environment instead of lying down in the snow? You can make a green bough bed as an insulating mattress to lift you off the frozen landscape. Shake off the snow from any available evergreen boughs, and break them loose or saw them off. In the deep cold, the water in these branches will be frozen and you might be surprised how easy it is to break them. Try bending each branch back toward the trunk to break it, or cracking it and peeling it away from the tree. Once you have a large pile of evergreen boughs, lay them out to make your mattress. Set the boughs down in pairs at right angles to each other. Repeat the pattern and overlap for the full length you will need. Test it by lying on it during construction, checking for thin spots that need more insulation. Repeat your layer building until you have a mattress that is several inches thick—even when compressed under your weight.

Don't Eat Snow for Hydration

Every school kid knows better than to eat the "yellow snow," but many people are often confused about eating snow for hydration in a winter emergency. As we discussed at the beginning of the chapter, snow does contain 5 to 10 percent water, and we need that vital resource every day. But snow is also full of freezing cold air, which is not something we want to take into our bodies when we are stuck in the frigid wilderness. It may all seem like a smart idea when the first mouthful of snow turns into a liquid in your parched mouth, but then you get hit with the brain freeze, and you start to chill your body's core if you keep going beyond that. Because of the high air content of snow, you'd have to eat many quarts of it to get one quart of melted water in your belly, and this is a losing proposition. You'd freeze to death in your attempt to avoid death from dehydration. Just remember, if it's cold enough for snow, it's cold enough for hypothermia, and that's not the time or place to be eating frozen treats.

Build a Snow Melting Rig

So you've been advised against eating snow for a water source in cold conditions, but how *do* you get a water supply when the local waterways have turned into ribbons of solid ice? For those who happen to have a large cooking pot

(continued next page)

and a roaring fire, you can fill the pot with snow and melt to create drinking water. If the snow is fresh, it should be safe enough to drink once the snow becomes liquid water. If the snow is old—or you are not sure about its cleanliness— boil the water for five minutes for an additional margin of safety. And if you don't happen to have a large pot, there's a snow melting trick that works with a few sticks, a fire, and a smaller container to catch the water. It's called a "Finnish marshmallow" and the "snowman's head," due to its occasional resemblance to the same. Make a large snowball with packable snow on the end of a three-pronged stick. Prop it up near your fire, using a forked stick or some other sturdy support system. The water will begin to melt from the snow and flow to the lowest point underneath the snowball. Once the water begins dripping, set your container underneath and collect your drinking water. To keep producing, just pack more snow around the existing snowball and keep your fire burning brightly.

7
Advanced Shelters

When you need something a little larger and more durable than a pile of leaves for a shelter, take a page from our predecessors and consider building a more complex and long-lasting home in the wilderness. Various styles of cabins, shacks, and huts have been around for thousands of years, and if you possess some basic building skills, you might be able to stick around longer, too. Of course, building a more substantial structure is a major drain on calories, but for a long-term survival situation, it starts to make a lot of sense. In a larger shelter, you'll have room for sleeping and storage. You may even be able to integrate a hearth or fireplace for interior heating in cold weather. This means that your dwelling will provide greater warmth and comfort, the ability to work indoors during bad weather, and the space to store all kinds of useful resources.

So what kind of structure would be best? The different regions and environments that we might attempt to use for survival can give us a wide range of building materials. These various materials, in turn, can lead us toward specific shelter types that suit the season, weather, and location. For example, a rocky and tree-less desert area may not be a viable log cabin location, but it could be the perfect place for a small hut with stone walls. Similarly, the swamp would be a terrible place for an in-ground shelter of any kind, yet it's the perfect place for a raised shelter. By letting the available resources and the local conditions act as your guide, you'll have the best chance of making a structure that will fit both the landscape and your needs in a survival setting.

Try a Tree House

At some point, most kids ask for a tree house. It's a fun place to play, and on some level, we seem to instinctively feel safer up there. Once the years pass by and we get a bit older, we all seem to forget about this lofty lodge—though we shouldn't. In a jungle setting, where the ground is roiling with snakes, spiders, scorpions, and other biting creatures after sundown, getting off the ground can take on a whole

new level of importance. The simplest approach is to find a tree with existing branches that can support the shelter. Two matching lateral branches would be ideal, but failing that, use one and create a matching support with two heavy forked posts and a beam between them. Cut a large number of straight wrist-thick poles that can span the gap between the lateral supports and lash them in place. When poles are scarce or cutting them is too hard, use your thicker poles where the span is widest and use the thinner poles over short spans. Make your work easier by lashing together a ladder—for use while building and to gain access to the shelter. Make your dwelling safer by adding a safety rail around the edge of the platform. If you happen to have mosquito netting, drape your bug net over the platform to defend against biting insects. For other biting creatures, like snakes and rats, tie bundles of thorny branches in rings around posts and the main tree trunk. This won't stop ants and spiders, but it can discourage larger animals from joining you in your tree fort. Add a tarp roof, or even a thatched roof, and call it home.

Build a Jungle Hut

When you can't find the right tree branches for a jungle tree house, a small hut on stilts could be your next best bet. This will be more labor-intensive than a tree house platform, but your raised hut can also have more features, including a roof and a fireplace. Begin by marking off the shelter "footprint" on the ground. Continue by sinking some posts into the ground or cutting the tops off small-to-medium-sized trees so that they act as posts. Since you probably won't find trees growing in the exact pattern you want, you can combine some cut-off trees and a few planted posts to get the right configuration. A few short posts can support the beams that will hold up the floor, while a few taller beams can support roofing components. Next, you'll want to cut a few logs to become your floor joists and roof beams. Secure these into position with sturdy rope and strong knots. Lash some thick poles across the floor joists to make a platform and build a ladder to climb onto it. Construct a lean-to–style roof with thatching or debris. Make some woven or stacked log walls to block the wind, and you're almost done. Add a fire to your wooden shelter by using logs to create a frame, then filling it with mud or sand as a fire-proof buffer.

Add Some Thatching

The thatched roof is not unique to any culture or time period. In fact, we see this roofing style in most places with abundant grasses and similar vegetation. Made for many millennia, thatching techniques are as diverse as the materials available and the people who wove them. Yet despite these differences, most thatch roof construction is performed the same way. First, consider the shelter frame you are building. The steeper the angle of the roof, the better the thatching will work. Even though shelter frameworks can be any shape or size, steep roof architecture is vital to the effectiveness of thatching. The second feature in common is the placement of thatching materials. Grasses and similar plants are used upside down (compared to the way they grew), and leaves (like palm, for example) are placed so that the leaflet tips point down instead of upward. This placement allows rain to be channeled down through the thatch materials and out toward the edge of the roof. If the thatching is thick enough and the roof pitch is steep enough, the water will run off

(continued next page)

rather than drip through. The third factor for weatherproofing is secure attachment. If cordage is abundant, you can tie a wide range of grassy plant material to the horizontal roofing members. Vegetation such as rushes, reeds, cattails, and sedges can be found in wet areas. Field grasses and assorted weeds can be used in drier areas as a thatched roof. When cordage is not plentiful, use pairs of sticks to clamp the thatching materials together. This will only require a few cord pieces or flexible bark strips to sandwich the thatching securely and a few more bits of cord to tie the sticks in place. Particularly long grasses can even be bent in half and tied around the horizontal roofing members. And when all else fails, you can skewer large leaves onto sticks to create a cordage-free thatching option. Just keep safety in mind, remembering that dry thatch is very flammable!

Tree Cutting Safety

When you are cutting firewood or dropping trees to build a shelter, there is a very real set of risks to you, as well as a serious risk for nearby people, animals, and property. There's a reason why dead tree tops are called "widow makers." These tops can drop on an unlucky wood cutter and turn someone back home into a widow (or widower). But getting smashed by a snapped-off tree top isn't your only concern. There are other risks with cutting trees, and several ways to limit those risks.

- Remember that no two trees are identical. You'll need to take a good, long look at each tree before you make the first cut.
- When you are looking at a tree, check it for cracks, rotten tops, or dead branches overhead. Also, pay close attention to which direction a tree is leaning.
- Don't try to fight a leaning tree or the wind. When there's more weight on one side or the wind is pushing it, you'll be hard-pressed to make it fall the other way. You should also rethink the felling of trees on windy days.
- Work safer. Cut away any brush or vines in the work area around the tree trunk. You'll also want to clear your escape routes before you try to drop a tree.
- Ensure that the area is clear of people and pets before you start cutting.
- Wear protective equipment and don't work alone. Have someone nearby, but out of the reach of the falling tree.

Dig a "Scout" Pit

Although the origin of this shelter is a little murky, its usefulness in a hostile situation is clear. The scout pit is a hidden shelter built down into the ground, rather than above ground. Structurally similar to a snow trench, this haven is dug into the dirt and camouflaged to blend into the landscape. When properly built, the "scout" can hide inside this secret shelter, and the "bad guy" could even walk across the shelter roof without realizing that anyone was underneath their feet. To build this specialized shelter, start by choosing an area with good drainage and soil that is easy to dig. (You don't want to create this in a low lying area where the pit could fill with water, or in rocky soil that's impossible to dig.) Resist the urge to place it in a ready-made low spot, like a ditch or dry stream bed. Those spots will flood with any significant rainfall. Mark out the dimensions for the pit, a little wider and longer than you would be lying down. Remove the top six inches of soil and set it aside, ideally on a tarp to avoid leaving a raw dirt patch on the ground. Keep this nearby, as it will be needed later to cover the top of the scout pit roof. Keep digging the pit until it is "hip deep" to the user. Next, cut a ledge into the dirt around the rim of the pit. This should be about six inches deep and six inches wide, and this recess will hold the small logs, which will make up the shelter roof. After the digging is complete and the bulk of the dirt has been removed from the area, cut a number of logs that are the width of the pit, including the shelf. These should be between three and six inches wide for the strength to support several inches of dirt as well as a person or two standing on the roof. Thinner logs or poles won't always support the weight, and even if they did, they would create a "bouncing" sensation when someone observant walks over the pit.

Fill the pit with dry debris for bedding and place the logs across the pit, settling them into the shelf area. Run these supports across the width of the pit, and leave a gap at around chest height for entry and exit. This entrance hole can be bolstered by adding a few short poles on the sides, lengthwise with the pit. Next, cover the shelter roof with several inches of vegetation (dead leaves are ideal), then add the topsoil you reserved. Cut or find one or more planks of wood to act as a trap-door cover. Sprinkle a layer of twigs and debris over the entire area and use some sticky pine sap or a similar adhesive to stick debris to your trapdoor cover.

Create an Earth Lodge

Certain Native American nations and other far-off cultures have built dwellings from the very earth itself (and still occasionally do). These soil-covered homes were once a common sight in America's heartland, but the building technology can still be a fit for drier locations and desert climates. Begin by planting four strong posts into the ground and carefully securing four log beams atop the posts. These should be spiked into position with heavy iron or steel spikes to prevent them from shifting. These are literally the backbone of the shelter, and if they fail, they can bring the whole roof down onto the occupants. Once the posts and beams are secure, surround the log "cube" with roof poles so that it resembles something like a teepee. Leave a gap in the wall and construct a tunnel-like entrance through the wall. Cover the exterior with a thick layer of grass for insulation and to keep the dirt from falling through. Finish the structure with packed soil, leaving a hole in the roof for smoke to escape if you plan to burn a fire inside.

Build Your Own Cabin

This pioneer palace can be a sturdy choice for a wilderness shelter, and this is hardly new technology. You don't have to be a Colonial American hero like Daniel Boone to build a cabin from logs in a forest

or woodland environment. People have used logs to create homes all around the world, and with an ax, plenty of trees and a strong back, the log cabin is within your reach, too. By using thick building components like logs, you can take advantage of the tremendous strength and the insulating mass of large pieces of wood. Just do yourself a big favor and make it a small cabin.

Grab Your Tools

At a minimum, you'll need a sharp ax and something to measure the logs. Other very helpful tools and supplies include a drawknife for cutting off bark, hand saws for notching, a level, a heavy hammer, and some steel spikes to secure cabin corners. Shingles or other roofing materials are also needed.

Plan the Build

You'll have two main options for easy cabin architecture. For a traditional look, you can sink two posts into the ground and run a beam between them to support an "A-frame" roof. The other option is to build one of your longer walls higher and create a relatively flat roof that leans. Either way, keep your cabin on the smaller side in order to work on roofing without a tall ladder.

Set the Walls

Start the build by setting logs horizontally, either with the corners notched or just overlapping (notched is much stronger and safer). Cut in a tiny door and a window or two, and fill any gaps between the logs with moss or a blend of mud and plant fiber. This is called chinking, and it will keep your heat in and keep the wind from blowing through the walls.

Create the Roof

If you think the walls need to be strong, consider the roof. There will be a tremendous amount of weight overhead, unless you use a tarp for a roof, and it needs to be well-built. Cut some stout poles to build your roof, then lash them in place or notch them so they stay in position. Cover the poles with vegetation, thatching, bark slab shingles, or anything else you have at your disposal. Start at the bottom edge of the roof, then work your way up to the peak.

Add a Chimney

Cabins aren't very warm without a fire inside, so building a sturdy chimney is another important feature. Some early American cabins featured chimneys built from small logs, stacked just like the cabin walls. These were heavily plastered in mud for partial fire-proofing, but they were still a serious fire hazard and should only be attempted in areas with no stone. A stone chimney is much safer and more durable. Just make sure that you keep all fires tiny to minimize your fire risks and build the majority of the chimney freestanding so that the chimney is not attached to the log wall higher up. This gap allows you to throw water between the chimney and log wall in the event of a chimney fire.

Construction Details

For the strongest possible cabin corners, corner notching is the way to go. The notches form a series of interlocking connections that essentially hold the cabin together. Depending on the tools you have available, there are dozens of different notch styles you can create, but here are the four easiest.

V-Notching: Using the same ax that dropped the trees, cut a ninety degree angle at the end of each log on one side. Then cut in a matching notch on the other side at each end. These must be carefully measured to line up, but they are easy to cut.

Square Notching: Harder to cut, but more forgiving if you make a mistake in measurement, square off each end of your logs and stack the corners.

Round Notching: By carefully marking the shape of the lower log onto the top one, you can roll it away, then cut away the wood and roll it back into position. If you did it right, it should lock down around the curvature of the log underneath.

(continued next page)

No Notching: The fastest method, though the least stable. Don't cut any notches in the corners. Leave your logs round, overlap them, and occasionally drive a spike down through the corner crossings to pin the logs together.

Tips for the Builder

Reading a few pages about cabin building is no substitute for working with logs in real life, and as you'll see, it's hard work, and mistakes are easy to make. Still, a few pro tips can shorten your learning curve.

Rough Openings: It's hard enough to put cabin walls together, and it's even harder when the walls have openings. Attempting to leave door and window openings during construction is unstable and dangerous. If you're lucky enough to have a chainsaw to cut your logs, use it to carve out door and window openings after the walls are finished and braced for structural strength.

Lay the Foundation: While logs can be used in contact with bare dirt, it's not always a great idea in wet areas (or in landscapes full of termites). You can try to use wood species that resist rot and bugs, like cedar and black locust, or you can use stone as a buffer between the soil and logs. Stone perimeter walls can be laid as a foundation for the log walls to rest upon. This doesn't block the most determined termites, but it does get the logs off the damp ground.

Alternate the Courses: Sometimes you spot a problem when it's too late to fix it. Since logs naturally taper, you'll have a

(continued next page)

thick end and a thin end on each and every log. If you don't alternate your log ends while building the walls, you'll soon find that you spent a lot of hard labor building a lopsided and unstable wall. Alternate the logs of each course and you'll avoid this irksome situation.

Build a Stone Hut

We saved the toughest build for the end of the chapter, and I can't recommend this structure for amateurs. Building a stone hut requires a backbreaking amount of work and at least a basic understanding of masonry. Without the proper structural support, the stones you've lifted could come crashing down on you, converting your hut into a tomb. That being said, necessity is the mother of invention, and given the need (and plenty of time and skill), I think the average person could figure it out. There are even some major benefits to this type of shelter. With regular roof maintenance, your stone hut may last for a very long time. It will also offer you greater defense against predatory animals. A stone hut could also allow for an indoor fire with a greater margin of safety than many other dwellings. Just remember that you were warned. This is potentially a dangerous structure, and it's a ton of work—literally, as you may have to move a ton of stone or more for even a tiny hut. What follows is a grossly oversimplified explanation of a complex and laborious shelter construction.

Choose a level building site, adjacent to a wealth of suitable stone. These rocks should be blocky, flat, square, or angular. A mountain of round river cobbles will be less stable and will not be likely to create a sturdy stone hut (without an abundance of cement, anyway). Mark off the ground to show the position and length of your walls. Choose your door location, too. Your door should be facing away from the

prevailing winds. Make sure to plan the height of your walls; they shouldn't be taller than you, especially if built from "dry" stone without any mortar. Remember to keep it small; you don't need to build a castle here. Use a blocky stone to pound the ground around your hut perimeter to compact the soil for more stable walls. Excavate any loose or soft soil and build up a "footer" of stone, if needed. Start stacking rocks, looking for the spot that each one fits best. Use little stones as a wall core material and to fill gaps. You can also blend mud and grass to make a crude survival cement to fill gaps. Keep the walls thicker at the bottom and thinner toward the top as you build up. For more stability, the walls should be leaning inward on both sides. Cap the walls with flat stones. Add wooden beams, roofing material, and your door. If you decide to go with windows, make them above the stone wall (not in it), since they will only weaken your stone work. Pack gaps with mud mortar, and enjoy your new home.

8

Shelter in Modern Emergencies

In the previous chapters, the subject matter wasn't too heavy. You get lost in the woods, it's not so bad, you build a shelter, and everything is going to be fine. In this chapter, however, things are going to take a turn for the worse. Here, we'll look at some other situations in which shelter is still one of your top survival priorities, but you'll have a lot of other issues to worry about in addition to shelter. In modern times, much of the world's population enjoys conveniences and technologies that would have boggled the minds of our primitive ancestors. But with an increasing reliance on fragile systems, we sometimes find ourselves doing without a luxury that we have come to believe is a necessity. Take electricity for example. Unless a person is connected to equipment that is keeping them alive, you can live without electricity. This life is much harder and less comfortable without it, but most of us won't drop dead if the lights go out. This does put us in an awkward spot, however, when we try to muddle along in the wake of a disaster that interrupts our routine and resources. For this reason, we've included a chapter in *The Ultimate Guide to Survival Shelters* on finding shelter in modern emergencies. Here, we'll go over your options for staying in a building without heat or cooling, how to take shelter in a car, building a refuge from plane wreckage, and even finding shelter in an urban survival setting. Survival is never just about "sticks in the woods." It's much more than that. Survival is about using the resources you have to make the necessities you need, and this can happen in any kind of environment or situation—not just getting lost in the woods.

Stay Cool

We often picture ourselves struggling to keep warm when we imagine a disaster survival setting, but what happens when the utilities go down and the weather is hot? In the summer season or a hot climate, finding a way to cool down can be almost as important as staying warm in a frosty setting. Here are some easy ways to keep your cool during a hot weather emergency.

Go Underground

It doesn't have to be a cave system or a secret underground complex to provide you with a cool shady refuge from the heat. Basements and building sub-levels are naturally cool in hot weather, thanks to the cool temperature of the earth. The actual soil temperatures will vary a lot throughout a continent, depending on your latitude, location, season, depth, and several other factors, but if you can find a way to get a few feet below the surface level, you'll find yourself in much cooler air. Soil temperatures are typically in the sixties across the southern US, in the fifties across the central band of states, and down in the forties in northerly states. Find a cool place underground, or even lie on a cool basement floor to conduct body heat away and find some respite from the hot weather.

Use Evaporation

Remember the methods for heat loss from Chapter One, "Understand the Threats"? They were radiation, convection, conduction, and evaporation. This last one concerns us now, as a method of cooling. By hanging up wet cotton sheets (thin ones, not quilts), and resting below those sheets, cooler air will naturally fall off them and drift down onto your resting place. For best effect, use a bit of rope to set up a clothesline and suspend your wet sheet across the rope like an "A-frame" tent. Make sure the sheet is secure, and crawl underneath. The air will be many degrees cooler under there, and you can remoisten the sheet as needed for continued cooling.

Make Your Own Heat

Whether you live in a townhouse, condo, apartment, or a mansion, losing your utilities during a cold weather emergency can leave you in a dangerous position. Of the annual hypothermia deaths in the United States, very few of these happen in the wilderness. Most of these sad losses occur among the homeless living in urban areas and to those living without winter heating. Even indoors, death from hypothermia is a real threat when the outside temperatures are sub-freezing and your normal heating options are down.

Gain Warmth from the Sun

Just as the sun warms our entire planet in the cold vacuum of space, the sun can also warm up small places—if you know where to go. In a cold weather catastrophe, managing the warmth of the sun could be your new "day job," and it's a safe and easy way to get warm. On the high end, you could plan ahead for a cold weather utility interruption by adding a solar heating array to the roof of your home or business, but this isn't a plan that many can afford. What we all can do is something much more basic. Take advantage of the assets you already have in place. When the blizzard clouds have passed and the sun returns, you can easily utilize passive solar heat during daylight hours when you stay in a smaller room with south-facing windows, the more windows the better (south-facing when you're in the Northern Hemisphere; you'll want north-facing windows below the equator). Gain more heat by placing dark-colored objects in the direct sunlight. You can drape dark blankets over the furniture and lay darker rugs on the floor to capture the maximum amount of heat from the available sunlight. You'll quickly see that the more light you have coming into the room and the more dark colors you place in that light, the more heat you will gain. And when the sun starts to get low and the heat dwindles, cover those windows with several layers of thick drapes or find some improvised insulation (like cardboard) to block the room's heat loss through the windows at night.

Sticks and Stones Will Heat Your Home

If you can't put a fire inside the dwelling, try putting it outside and bringing in the heat. How is this possible? Since we're only after the heat (not necessarily the flames and smoke), it's possible to store heat in certain objects and then bring them into an enclosed space to provide portable radiant heat. Still lost? Then here's how you can also turn rocks and bricks into space heaters.

The first thing you'll need to do is create a heat-proof platform in the room you intend to heat. If you have a fake fireplace or one that's not working, your brick or stone hearth is usually a fine place to set the hot objects. If not, build a platform from bricks, cinderblocks, or flat stones lying on the floor. Next, collect some bricks or a few rocks from a dry location (waterlogged stones can explode when heated, so avoid them). Once you have your bricks or stones, fire up your propane grill or build a fire on the ground. Toss your rocks or bricks in the grill or campfire and heat them for about forty-five minutes. Scoop them out with a shovel or pitchfork and knock off any embers or sparks from the bricks or rocks. Place the bricks or rocks in a large stainless steel cooking pot. Don't use other types of pots. Non-stick coatings may burn up, giving off noxious chemicals, and galvanized buckets will release toxic vapors when heated. Just use an ordinary steel pot. Wearing thick gloves and being extremely careful as you walk, bring the pot full of heated rocks or bricks inside the dwelling and place it on your fireproof platform. Rewarm the rocks or bricks every few hours as needed.

Plan Ahead with Heaters

You have no one to blame but yourself if you live in a place that suffers cold temperatures and frequent power outages. Plan for this annual threat by investing in a backup heat source.

Kerosene Heater: These don't smell particularly pleasant, and they do give some people a headache, nevertheless, kerosene heaters are simple to use, and they can be found in models that are designed for indoor use (read the label carefully before purchase). Just make sure you stock up on several days' worth of kerosene before the bad weather hits. Kerosene can be purchased at many gas stations, particularly in colder climates, and it can even be used in certain lamps for emergency lighting. Don't forget to crack a window just a little bit for adequate ventilation.

Wood Stove: In locations with plenty of firewood, installing a wood-burning stove can be an excellent backup for winter heating (or your day-to-day heating). A properly installed stove can safely heat a smaller home or several rooms in a larger house. You can even cook on the hot stove top. Stoves can be a significant expense, and all combustion sources represent a fire hazard, but once you've handled the initial cost, wood stoves can be an inexpensive heating option for a home or building—especially if you are able to cut your own firewood.

Propane Heater for Indoor Use: Certain small propane heaters are designed with "low oxygen cut-off" sensors and other safety features that greatly reduce the risk of carbon monoxide poisoning. These are capable of connecting to small propane cylinders (like the green ones for camping stoves) or on larger propane bottles (like your hamburger grill tanks). When placed in a fire-proof area, like the middle of a tile floor, they are surprisingly safe for heating closed spaces, with just a slight amount of ventilation.

Limit Your Danger With Emergency Heating

It doesn't make much sense to trade one threat for a different one, and setting your home on fire during a winter emergency might be just as dangerous as hypothermia. Do whatever you can to stay safe and be efficient in your attempt to improvise heating in a frosty situation.

Don't Overdo It
If you attempt to heat your entire dwelling with improvised heat sources, you're wasting your time. Just focus on heating one small room with a low ceiling in your house or other shelter site. This smaller room will be easier to heat and it can serve as your main living area during the emergency. Don't try to get every room in your home comfortable again.

Remember to Allow Airflow
When we "batten down the hatches" of our dwelling, this is our natural response to cold. You're trying to stop air

(continued next page)

leaks and drafts. But when doing this, we also block off fresh air, which is critical with combustion-based heating. Kerosene heaters and other "indoor safe" heaters still need air, so crack a window in the room where the heat source is being used. Never use an outdoor propane heater, hamburger grill, or a gas kitchen stove as a heat source; they are all capable of killing your family with carbon monoxide poisoning.

Limit the Candles

They certainly are romantic, and even more problematic. For lighting, a carefully-managed candle or two can create a lot of light. But if you try to use dozens of them as a heat source, you're just begging for a house fire in addition to the emergency that knocked out your heat. It's a serious fire hazard to have candles burning unattended, in large numbers, or around young children or energetic pets who might knock them over. Also, make sure you have a working smoke alarm with a carbon monoxide detector.

Staying Warm in the Office

We're not all lucky enough to get caught at home with all of our supplies during a cold weather emergency, and when the power goes out, your whole workplace may be without heat. Luckily, there are several things you can do, prior to burning all your paperwork in a garbage can for warmth. As we mentioned earlier, you and your chilly co-workers could take advantage of the natural warmth of the sun by getting out of those windowless offices and large drafty rooms full of cubicles and seeking shelter in a small office with south-facing windows (in

the northern hemisphere). If that isn't an option, try the basement or a sublevel in the building, where the warmth of the earth will be noticeable. When neither of these strategies is available, consider using insulation for warmth. Choose a small space and pack it with insulating materials. Build up insulation on the floor by stacking cardboard or foam as a warm "mattress." Then create a nest around it with bubble wrap, crumbled paper, or anything else that offers insulation value. It's all about dead air space. If agreeable, build this nest for several people, since the extra body heat will add up quickly. It's not very glamorous or heroic, but by emulating the humble animals who build nests to stay warm, we can stay warm, as well.

Carbon Monoxide Kills

It's tasteless, colorless, odorless, and lethal, and in an emergency, you have enough to worry about without dealing with carbon monoxide. Yet every year, creative but uneducated people die (and sometimes even perish with their whole family) due to carbon monoxide poisoning in homes. Maybe someone's burning a fireplace or stove with a blocked chimney, or some creative survivor drags a propane grill into the living room for heat. What started as an attempt to produce heat during a utility outage ends up being a greater threat than the emergency itself. As any combustion occurs in a confined space, even something as big as a house, the oxygen levels drop. As soon as a fire doesn't have enough oxygen available to produce carbon dioxide, the struggling fire begins to produce carbon monoxide. When breathed in, this gas takes the place of oxygen in your blood. The results are usually drowsiness and irritability, and if you succumb to the temptation for a nap, you're likely to die of suffocation in your sleep. ONLY use heating products indoors if they are designed for indoor use. These devices usually include a low oxygen shutoff mechanism. You'll also need fresh air, even when it's cold outside. It's better to feel a draft from a window than to feel the guilt of killing your family with carbon monoxide.

Plane Crash Shelter

While plane crashes are very rare occurrences, small aircraft aren't exactly known for being a "hazard free" way to get around town. When a mechanical malfunction occurs, the situation can take a

literal "nose dive" in a hurry. These emergencies can pop up quickly and without warning. And if your luck is mixed (you were in a plane crash, but can walk away from the wreck), your troubles aren't over yet. In a remote area, help may be delayed, and if the crash didn't kill you, hypothermia still might. In a wilderness setting, you could certainly fall back on the shelters you'd build from natural materials. Or you could take advantage of the abundant resources from the plane to construct a survival shelter for yourself and any survivors.

Shelter in the Airplane Cabin

Once you have accounted for everyone onboard (survivors report that it's easy to overlook a missing crew member or passenger while the adrenaline is pumping) and you've dealt with the invariable injuries as best as possible, it's time to get to work on the survival priority of shelter. When a plane doesn't set down too hard, you can sweep over the aircraft inside and out, and from nose to tail. Carefully inspect the cabin to make sure that the structure is intact, and to make sure that you don't smell any fuel or spot any leaking fluids. If everything checks out, your simplest shelter is the cabin of the plane itself. Again, only take shelter if it seems safe. Just one leaking hydraulic fluid line or gas line can lead to a catastrophic fire or explosion, killing everyone who was lucky enough to survive the crash. Never take shelter in a downed aircraft if you even suspect that fluids have spilled. Not only are these liquids toxic, but hydraulic fluid has also been known to spontaneously combust. If you detect a leaking fluid or simply suspect one, build your survival camp at least 100 feet away from the plane to avoid injury from a fire or explosion.

Recycle the Wreckage

You walked away from the crash landing but the plane is broken into pieces? Count your blessings and then get to work scavenging any fuel-free plant components that can be converted into a shelter. Largely made from aluminum and other lightweight materials, sections of airplane wing and tail may be surprisingly easy to drag across the ground and prop up against logs, rocks, or other supports. These can be cobbled together into a quick lean-to shelter or some other shelter styles that suit the nature of the aircraft component. For example, you can use smaller pieces of metal as roof shingles, or use bigger sections as complete roofing panels. You can also use random pieces in wet environments to get you up off the damp ground. This can create a problem, since metal is a terrible insulator and lying on cold metal will conduct away your precious body heat. If conditions are cold at your crash site, even just at night, you can scavenge some insulating materials to go between your body and the chilly metal. Make a floor covering from seat cushions, carpet material, or anything else that insulates you from the cold.

Use the Raft for a Shelter

Large to mid-size aircraft already have a great shelter onboard, one that's capable of being moved away from the potentially explosive plane wreckage. It's the life raft, and if this "pop-up" shelter survives the crash along with you, drag it 100 feet away from the plane and pull the cord. Life rafts normally save people after a water landing, but they can also save you on dry land, if they can be located in the debris. A big rubber raft with a canopy can provide excellent coverage from the rain and wind, and even if your raft lacks a canopy, it can still be used as a refuge. Just flip it over and use the raft as a roof. Once the raft is inflated, tie it down to keep the raft in place if the conditions get windy (rafts tend to blow away). Don't forget the added bonus hidden inside most rafts—it's very likely to have a survival kit inside. This pack will generally contain food, water, a locator beacon, and a host of other lifesaving supplies. And as a bonus feature, rafts are usually constructed from high visibility colors to make it easier for search and rescue teams to locate. Nothing says "look over here" like a big red, orange, or yellow raft lying in the wilderness. To finish off this unexpected shelter, fill the space under your raft shelter with scavenged insulation and your shelter will protect you from the cold as well as rain, wind, and all the other elements.

Hide from the Heat

Survival shelters aren't just necessary in the cold. They can be lifesavers in the heat, as well. In a hot and sunny environment, you may need a shade-producing shelter to keep you cool. You may find protection from the heat in the shade under the airplane wings, or you may have to build something from the pieces. Start by collecting any space blankets, regular blankets, trash bags, carpeting, or similar materials you can find. Using cord or duct tape, secure them over any kind of framework (like a stick tripod) to make a rough and ugly version of a tent. Crawl inside and let these materials work their magic, interrupting the sunlight and creating a shady spot to rest. With the sunlight blocked, this shelter will be much cooler than the surrounding sunbaked landscape.

Don't Wander Off

One massive mistake that many plane crash survivors make is wandering away to "find help" in the middle of nowhere. And in these remote areas, the decision is even worse when a survivor decides to wander off alone. Don't let this idea get into your head. It's far smarter to stay near the plane and improvise some kind of camp near the crash site. This allows you to take advantage of the plane's visibility and its abundant resources. Your rescuers will also have a much easier time spotting a downed aircraft crash site than an individual waving his arms in a forest. Just stay put.

Urban and Suburban Shelters in a Crisis

Here's a little scenario for you. You work in a city and live in the suburbs. It's the end of a long day of toil and late in the afternoon, a controversial event touched off rioting within the city limits. You try to head home on mass transit, along with a hoard of people trying to flee. The buses and metro have stopped running, and there isn't a cab to be seen. Several hours pass and darkness falls. You head back to your workplace but the building is locked. Major roads are gridlocked during this failure of civility, so even if you had your vehicle, you couldn't drive it anywhere. In some situations, you may find that driving your vehicle or taking public transportation isn't a viable option to escape an area in turmoil. Sure, you could try to walk home during the event if you live nearby, but finding a place to hole up for the night might be the safest thing you can do. But where do you turn?

Book a Room

I know it's not as gritty as building an urban fortress out of refrigerator boxes, but it's a cleaner and safer choice. It's a long shot; however, you might just find a room at a local hotel that will let you in. Don't expect a warm welcome, as they will probably not be eager to open the door (or even come near the door). But if you can get anyone to answer the front desk phone or come to the door, you might just be able to spend the night in a locked building and inside your own locked room.

Hide in the Park

The homeless people know how to stay warm. Follow their lead by getting off the street and hiding out in some secluded corner of a park or some other green space in the city limits. Of course, this takes you away from law enforcement, so make sure you aren't being followed and do your best to disappear without a sound into an overgrown area. Watch where you step when walking through the brush, weeds, and woods, since these areas are often littered with human excrement and heroin needles. Don't build a fire, put up a tent, or perform any other "camping" activities. Prowlers will see you before you can see them. You don't want to give away your position. Just crawl into your sleeping bag (if you have one) and get a little rest. Better yet, wear enough outerwear, like thick coats and insulated pants, so that you can simply lie down on a sleeping pad or pile of leaves in your clothing (while still wearing any backpack or gear you might carry), and sleep with your boots on, too. This way, you ready to run at a moment's notice.

Find a Crawlspace

Lots of buildings, both residences and businesses, have crawlspaces underneath. These are hardly desirable accommodations, sharing the dark dirty space with spiders, roaches, and rats, but if it keeps you from being beaten to death by marauders, they're better shelter than you might expect. When you happen to locate a crawlspace door that isn't locked (or bears a lock you can break), you'll have access to a place that is out of the weather and off the beaten path for most people. Like the park, make certain that no one sees you enter the crawlspace area. If the door or panel swings inward, you can actually lean up against it to rest or sleep. This way, if anyone tries to enter, they'll wake you by pushing on the door. You can also consider piling up some trash bags around the entry to conceal it (especially if you had to break the lock and the damage is obvious). On the bright side, you're out of the weather and very few people would go under there; but on the downside, there's probably only one way in or out, so you could potentially be trapped.

Use An Abandoned Building

These are creepy places, that's for sure, but they may get you out of the weather. It might be worth your time to check out abandoned homes, trailers, and buildings as potential sites for a few hours of shelter. These places are seldom unoccupied for long periods, and often used as a haven for drug use and those down on their luck, but you may be able to find a structure or an area in a building that can be fortified. For example, you may find an abandoned house in an urban area, and it may provide shelter in the attic. Pull down the ladder, cut off the string that you used to pull it down, and head on up there. Find a way to secure the trap door further, and it would be very hard for anyone to follow you up there (without making any noise, anyway). Outbuildings, sheds, and other small buildings may also provide a place to stay. You may end up with company in an attic, basement, factory office, or similar refuge if likeminded people seek shelter in the building. You may also end up being trapped in there, if people with less friendly intent take up residence in the structure.

Dumpster Dive

Most of us would rather be in the most spider-packed crawlspace than crawl into an urban dumpster, but consider this—not every dumpster is as bad as you might imagine. Before you jump headfirst into a random dumpster, stop to check the business that uses it (and never *jump* into any dumpster; climb in carefully). A dumpster full of dangerous material (like the trash dumpster behind the glass-cutting shop) isn't likely to be a safe or pleasant refuge. But the dumpster behind a department store may be full of packing material and even a few bits of discarded clothing (they often throw out sun-faded clothing from window displays). The dumpster behind the Bath & Body Works may be loaded with sweet-scented cardboard and bubble wrap packaging, which you could make into a fine set of bedding. The upside to dumpster diving is that you're out of the weather when hiding inside. And the main problem with this abode is that most dumpsters contain some nasty waste. Even in a "nice" dumpster, you'll probably have rats and roaches for company. And if trash service is still working during the civil unrest event, you could wake up by being turned upside down and dumped into the trash truck.

Take Shelter in a Vehicle

If you get stuck somewhere with your vehicle, it may make sense to stay with the car and use it for shelter. You may also find someone else's car (risky) that could serve in a pinch. As a shelter, most vehicles have limited interior space, and they can roast you in hot weather and freeze you in the cold. Even so, if you can find an unlocked car in a parking lot, someone may come through looting cars and you'll have to deal with that threat. A better location for sheltering in a car that isn't yours is a junkyard. Climb in, lock the doors, and get some rest until it's time to move on. Vehicles offer you a wind-proof, rain-proof shelter, and a little bit of security. If possible, select a car in an out of the way spot. Better yet, choose one that doesn't appear desirable or look like

it would contain anything valuable inside. You'll need plenty of insulating material to stay warm in there during cold weather (the metal vehicle body doesn't offer much insulation on its own). You can always keep an eye out for an upgrade, like a van or trailer—which could act as a more spacious shelter. As long as you don't damage any doors or windows to gain entry, the vehicle can protect you from wind and rain. You may be able to lock it for a little security, and if the vehicle runs, you may be able to run the engine occasionally for heat (but only if you know the exhaust is clear; an exhaust pipe buried in snow, slush, mud, or water will cause carbon monoxide to back up into the vehicle cabin, which can cause suffocation. Cold and rain aren't the only elements you might face in a survival situation that involves a vehicle. The heat can come into play as well, and the same metal frame that can be so cold in the winter will turn into an oven in the summer heat. The interior temperatures of many vehicles can exceed 130 degrees Fahrenheit in the hot summer sun. This is well above the range that can give you a heat-related illness like heatstroke. So instead of staying inside the car, park it over a ditch or low spot in the ground (to create more ground clearance) and lay down in the shade underneath the vehicle. This can afford you some protection until the temperatures drop enough to sit inside the vehicle once again.

Be Adaptable

Survivors are adaptable, and the more you open yourself up to the possibilities, the better your chances will be in most cases. There is a slight problem when you expand your options. Hick's law, named after British psychologist

(continued next page)

William Edmund Hick, states that a greater number of choices and options will slow down your reaction time. But this matters more in split-second emergency situations (like self-defense) than it does in shelter building. As we've said throughout the book, you typically have hours of survival time in a cold weather exposure event, and spending a few extra minutes deciding which shelter to use will not have much impact on your outcome. That being said, it's usually a smart idea to embrace our natural flexibility as humans. If you needed an urban shelter for just one night, maybe a giant trash bag is all you need. One of those huge appliance boxes or wooden crates could also pass for a temporary shelter. You might seek shelter underground, in a place like a service tunnel, which benefits from the natural warmth of the earth, or you may go up high—a rooftop could get you away from floodwaters. Being open to the possibilities, you may even stumble upon some completely unexpected shelter. Analyze the environmental conditions you are trying to defend against and be creative in the way you minimize their harmful impact. When it's raining, find a way to block it. When it's cold, take advantage of insulation and heat sources. When you feel threatened, get to a place that's defensible. The concept of "shelter" can mean many different things across the spectrum of survival situations, but at the heart of it all, you're simply identifying the threat and discovering a path to defeat it.

Create a Barricade Situation

Push can turn to shove in the blink of an eye during the unpredictable violence that civil unrest can bring. A protest or a large event can turn into window breaking and looting, and once that starts, the fire setting and violence may quickly follow. It's a sad truth that there are always a few "bad guys" in every group of people, and when a mass of unruly people forms, some will have darker objectives than just smashing a few shops. When something like a riot occurs and you're at the office, get together with your coworkers, and especially any security personnel, to have a quick discussion about who is staying in the building and who is going. Once you've determined which people are staying, have a lengthier talk about the possibilities for tightening security around and inside the building. For example, when taking refuge in a huge multi-story building, it's just not practical to "board up" all the windows and doors at ground level, but think about a choke point inside the building which would block intruders. This could mean blocking stairway doors or even cutting the power to disable the elevators. The important thing to remember is that you don't want to become imprisoned yourself. Have one or more emergency exit for your group, should the building be breached or a fire started inside or outside of the building. Get creative, and you might be surprised how easy it can be to barricade yourself. Try using filing cabinets, desks, and furniture to cover windows and block single

(continued next page)

doors. Tie the door handles together on double doors using extension cords or cables. Just make sure you leave yourself at least one emergency exit, since the barricading of all entry and exit points can turn your shelter into a place where you're trapped.

9

Make Any Shelter Better

Throughout the course of this book, you've seen how to make shelters from many of the different natural materials that can be sourced in the wild. You've also seen how to use modern materials like tarps and vehicles to find a haven from the bad weather. In total, this motley assortment of shanties and shelters is incredibly diverse, though all of these different dwellings have one thing in common: They can all be improved upon. Since exposure to the elements is your biggest threat in an outdoor emergency, a "good" shelter should never be considered "good enough." In this final chapter, we'll look at some of the different ways you can improve any shelter. We can't expect to build the world's most perfect shelter in the first few hours of an emergency setting, and then never work on it again. There will always be more work ahead, providing upkeep and maintenance on the shelter, and hopefully you'll have a shot at improving the dwelling, as well. This should make sense, when you consider the modern home in which you dwell. There's always some kind of chore list hanging around, and there's usually a wish list of home improvement items, too. There will always be gutters to clean and bugs to spray, and survival living has its own list of chores. You may find that your walls and roof aren't thick enough (and you'll usually find this out the hard way—when the rain leaks in). You may find that your bed won't allow much sleep. You may even find that you're not the only creature living in the shelter. From insulation to lighting, from predator defense to bug-repelling, there's always room for improvement—even when your shelter only has one room.

Add Some Warmth

While cooling down or beating the bugs may be important facets of survival shelter living, few modifications seem as important as keeping warm. To that end, there are two main ways to get the job done: by insulating better and by supplementing our body warmth with outside heat sources.

Build An Insulating Floor

The ground may be the foundation for everything we build, but when it's cold and damp, it can be a hypothermia-inducing mattress of death. Block the cold and moisture in many different shelters by adding a layer of vegetation or bark as a floor covering. It doesn't take much to achieve a drier and warmer floor, and this insulation can even pass for bedding in your shelter. Materials that naturally lie flat are a great choice. These can be broken chunks and slabs of dead bark (their corky composition is very insulating). Dead leaves, pine needles, and grass stalks will also work well. Just remember that dead, dry plant materials are a fire hazard, and you'll want to limit your use of fire in and around a shelter that has flammable flooring material.

Put Extra Blankets to Work

In a disaster setting or power outage, you can use the warmth of the sun to heat up a room during a bright day, but how do you keep that heat in at night? Even the best windows are major points of heat loss in the modern home, and exterior walls are the second worst. If you want to "store" the heat you gained in the daytime, you'll need a strategy to limit the heat lost each night. Lucky for us, there's an easy way to reduce our heat loss in a modern home or business. By covering walls and windows with extra blankets, heavy drapes, or any other kind of improvised insulation, you hold in much more heat after sundown. There's a reason that castles were once adorned with tapestries and other wall hangings; they were nice to view, but more importantly, they helped cut down on drafts and provide insulation. You can adapt this concept even further, by hanging up blankets over openings that lack a door, or by stretching blankets across rooms to create a lower ceiling in order to reduce the size of the space you have to heat. And even if you are not heating with the sunlight through the windows, your modern tapestries will provide a helpful barrier to the cold—just what you need in a winter emergency.

Get Primitive

Our ancestors didn't have closed-cell foam camping pads to protect them from sleeping on the cold, wet ground. They had natural materials for bedding, and these things are still available for our use today.

(continued next page)

Stack Up Some Furs

When bears are not a concern, and you've managed to take a few big game animals, you can take a page from our ancestors' playbook and use furs and hides for bedding. This isn't safe or smart where grizzlies or black bears roam, but in other areas, soft warm furs can create both a mattress and covers. You don't even need to engage in the laborious process of tanning the hides. Scrape away the meat and fat, stretch them out to dry, and then stack them up for a bed. You can also mix in other materials—build a pile of vegetation and then top it off with furs and hides.

Weave a Sleeping Pad

When tall grasses and long cattail leaves are abundant, these can be woven into a very warm sleeping mat. All you need are the grassy materials, some cordage, and lots of patience. Collect a large volume of the plant materials, roughly the equivalent of two full garbage cans. Cut three or four lengths of cord, fifteen feet long each. Form a slender bundle of the grassy stuff, a little longer than your body is wide, and roughly two inches in diameter. Tie your cords around the bundle, evenly spaced down the length of the bundle. For each cord, tie it in the middle of the cord's length so you have two equal legs of cord from each tied spot around the bundle. Once all the cords are tied, tie another grass bundle beside the first grass bundle using the cordage that's hanging down from the first series of

(continued next page)

knots. It's as if you're tying together a log raft, but it's grass bundles instead. Continue adding more grass bundles and tying them beside the previous one, and soon you'll have a surprisingly warm sleeping mat. You can also roll it up for storage. It's like a primitive Therm-a-Rest pad.

Make a Heating Pit

Certain shelters have never been known for warmth. For example, tarp shelters offer no insulation to hold in body heat, but that doesn't mean they need to be frigid. You do have another way to heat these living and sleeping areas besides insulation, and that is an in-ground heating pit. Start by gathering two rocks from a dry location (water-logged rocks can explode when heated). You'll need a flat rock to cover the pit and a good-sized rock that will be heated in the fire. Dig a small pit down into the dirt inside your shelter, just large enough to hold the rock you will be heating. This hole must be smaller than the rock you intend to use as a cover. Dig a small shelf around the edge of the pit so the cover rock can be recessed and level with the ground (to avoid a possible trip hazard). When you're ready for sleep, heat the stone that will go into the pit by placing it in the fire. You can also heat the lid stone slightly by propping it up near the fire. After an hour or so of heating, carry the hotter stone to the pit (a shovel with a long handle is your safest option for the transfer), and drop the stone in place. Cover the pit with the lid rock and enjoy several hours of heat.

Make the "Hot Rock" Mattress

Yes, this one is elaborate, and no, you can't easily couple it with a natural shelter (it's too much of a fire hazard to add this type of heated bed). Yet even with its flaws and limitations, the hot rock mattress is still something worth considering in certain cold and dry conditions.

In most deserts, it gets very cold at night, dropping as much as 50 degrees Fahrenheit from the daytime high. When there's little chance of getting rained upon and you're just looking for warmth, this might do the trick. With loose sand that's easy to dig, plenty of dry rocks, and abundant dead brush to burn, you'll have the ideal conditions to build a hot rock mattress. Get started by digging a shallow trench that is a little bit wider and taller than you would be when lying down. As you dig, pile up your loose dirt or sand alongside the trench for easy retrieval. This serves two purposes: The soil acts as a heat-reflecting wall while you're burning a fire in the trench, and it makes the soil readily available when it's time to cover the trench. Once excavated, place a layer of flat stones in the trench, filling it completely. Make sure to collect these rocks from a high, dry location, and do your best to arrange them so that they fit like a jigsaw puzzle (no big gaps or stone piles on top of each other). Ideally, the rocks should be flat, and it's fine if they are thicker than the depth of the trench; you'll be covering them with a layer of dirt and bedding. Once the rocks are in place, keep a fire burning on top of them for two to three hours. This will store a massive amount of heat in the rocks, and you can also take advantage of the fire during this heating process for cooking or boiling water. When the time is up, use a stick to rake away the coals and any burning wood to create a new fire beside the trench. Quickly move your loose dirt on top of the rocks to seal in the heat, making a dirt layer about four inches thick. Allow any moisture to steam out of the soil for ten or fifteen minutes, then add your bedding. This could be a pile of leaves or other vegetation, or you could use your normal outdoor bedding. As you lay there for the first few minutes, you will likely notice some "hot spots," which are areas where the dirt and/ or bedding are too thin. Strip these spots back to the dirt layer and add more dirt. Add more vegetation to buffer the heat. When built correctly, you'll have five to seven hours of glorious warmth conducting up into your bedding, and it will feel like you are lying on a warm sandy beach, even on a frosty desert night.

Bring in the Light

Few people would prefer to spend their time in a dark and gloomy space, so shelter elements that add more light can make the space much more livable.

Face the Right Direction

No matter which hemisphere you call home, get your bearings before you start building. Since the sun rises in the east, you'll typically want to face the doorway of your shelter to the east. This gives you a natural wakeup call with the morning sun, and it can also prevent bad weather from blowing in the door when the prevailing winds and storms come from the west.

There's No Reason You Can't Include a Window

When building igloos, snow caves, and quinzees, there's no rule that they have to be dark on the inside. Find a small sheet of clear ice (any shape), and incorporate it into a wall or roof to add a natural window. This addition can allow light to enter, making the space more useful during the daytime. It can also allow you to see outside, to check the weather, or look for threats before exiting. And when there is light inside the structure, the window will act as a beacon to help you to find your way back to the shelter in the dark.

Make Oil Lamps

Since campfires and igloos are not good friends, we can't exactly plop a fire down in the middle of any snow shelter to provide light during the nighttime hours. There's an easy solution to this issue when you need light without much heat, and most snow shelter cultures make use of this solution. Using a shell or stone bowl, some oil, and a plant fiber cordage as a wick, we can make a simple oil lamp for lighting. Add your oil (animal, vegetable, or mineral) to the fireproof container and lay a natural fiber wick into the oil, with about one inch of cordage sticking out. Light the oily wick with an open flame (this may take up to a minute with a fresh wick) and then your oil lamp will burn for a long time time, just like a candle.

Get Noticed

Shelters that are built with natural vegetation or camouflage tarps are very difficult to see from a distance. This can act against your best interests when a search and rescue party is looking for you, or you are simply trying to find your hut again after traveling away from it in conditions with poor visibility. To avoid blending into the surrounding landscape too well, mark the shelter with something that can easily be seen at a distance or in low light. A scrap of brightly colored cloth or plastic can be impaled on a tall stick and set out like a flag beside your shelter. Reflective items can be hung up in sunny areas, too. It would be a shame if the shelter that helped you survive a frigid night in the wilderness had such good camouflage that searchers couldn't find your camp in a rescue situation.

Repel the Critters

A great shelter for a person can also be a great shelter to the other creatures in that environment. What snakes wouldn't want to curl up in a warm pile of leaves on a cold night? And what cave-like structures wouldn't be viewed favorably by the local spider population? If you want to keep your shelter to yourself, you'll have to work toward that goal on a regular basis.

Reduce the Bug Population

Shelters made from natural vegetation are often full of insects and arthropods, since these creatures get scooped up along with the leaves, grasses, and pine needles. They may flee the shelter initially, due to the disturbance, but in warmer weather, they'll be back with all their friends in just a few days. Thankfully, there is a way to repel them initially and keep their population low. The shelter can be smoked to drive off these unwelcomed guests. You can do this by pulling out all bedding materials (especially those made with dead dry plants). Then collect some embers from a fire and place them in a fireproof container such as a huge shell, stone bowl, or metal pot. Crumble some dry rotten wood onto the embers and set the container on the bare ground inside the shelter. Cover the entry to the shelter and allow the smoke to fill the shelter for ten to fifteen minutes. Stay alert, since you technically have a fire inside your home, and make sure that the embers don't light anything on fire (since your hut is essentially a giant fire bundle). Perform this "smoking" procedure weekly in colder weather or every three days in warmer weather.

Scare Away Snakes

Snakes won't be any more fond of smoke than the bugs, but there's a simpler way to scare them off—disturbance. Snakes and other crawling creatures generally prefer to reside in quiet places with little disruption. But if you're tearing all your shelter bedding out every day and making a lot of commotion, they'll generally leave. Shake your plant material bedding out daily, not only to repel snakes, insects, and arthropods, but also to restore the loft of the bedding.

Pick a Practical Repellent

When we choose the right species of plants for our projects, we can often get an extra boost. By using the green branches of cedars and other insect-repelling trees in our shelter construction, these plants can naturally keep some of the bugs away. Just make sure you're not collecting anything that will bother you, too, like poison ivy or any of its kin.

Practice Makes Perfect

Since you never know when you'll find yourself in a wilderness emergency or a disaster setting, it makes sense to practice your skills in a safe training setting—before you actually need the skills. Your competence and confidence will only increase, and you may even learn some new tricks. This is important to note. The right time to try out some new shelter architecture or any other survival experiment is not during a real emergency. It's during the safety of your practice time. Practice making your shelter before you get into trouble, and you'll know exactly what to do when the time comes to build one for real.

In Conclusion

Now that we have reached the end, your head should be swimming with ideas for dozens of different survival shelters and dozens more ideas for techniques on how to make those shelters more effective and comfortable. As we sit in our climate-controlled homes, vehicles, and businesses, it can be hard to imagine how badly we need shelter. It's a resource that few people have to live without in modern society. That's why it's such a rude awakening for most people to find themselves in an emergency without a shelter when something unfortunate happens. But that sucker punch of fate won't hit you so hard now that you know you have a wealth of options for lodging in a survival situation. You're planning ahead and being prepared, and that should be applauded. Before we conclude the book, there's just one more thing I'd like to share with you about the importance of practicing these skills. There's a lot of information at your disposal now, and you've heard about some of my experiences in survival. Now it's time to make some experiences of your own. There's really no substitute for gaining your own first-hand experience in shelter building and other survival arts. Facts and figures can be useful, and learning from the mistakes and successes of others can help, but real survival wisdom comes from performing the tasks yourself and making your own memories about that skill. This wisdom just can't come from reading or watching videos. It comes from the memory of the things you tried, and, whether the skill worked or not, you've gained real experience that you can carry forward into the next situation. Don't just read about it, try it out!